First published in Great Britain in 1993 by
ANCHOR BOOKS
1-2 Wainman Road, Woodston,
Peterborough, PE2 7BU

Foreword

Anchor Books is a small press, established in 1992, with the aim of promoting readable poetry to as wide an audience as possible.

We hope to establish an outlet for writers of poetry who may have struggled to see their work in print.

Following our request in the National Press, we were overwhelmed by the response. The poems presented here have been selected from many entries. Editing proved to be a difficult and daunting task and as the Editor, the final selection was mine.

The poems chosen represent a cross-section of styles and content. They have been sent from all over the country, written by young and old alike, united in the passion for writing poetry.

I trust this selection will delight and please the authors and all those who enjoy reading poetry.

Michelle Abbott
Editor

Contents

Beware!

As you walk down the road
Do look out for Horny Toad,
Do not run away from him
his chance for friendship's very slim.
Once he was just like you
but for a small mistake in view,
He saw a witch, and forgot his teachings
on meeting witches, relay polite greetings,
He smirked, was rude and impolite,
so she gave him a terrible fright,
and now his life is to roam
looking for a Princess, and a home.
So on meeting witches, take good care
be polite, be kind, but most of all, *beware*
or you may find
Hedgerows for your home awhile.

Tricia Morgan

1

A World so Green

I see a world so green,
Beautiful countryside,
With birds that sing,
Too good to believe.

I see a world so dull and grey,
Smoke and poison.
Everywhere we go,
Something to expect wouldn't you say.

Why be so selfish and destroy,
Let our loved ones enjoy,
The world's beauty is for them to see,
So just let it always be!

Shelpa Ladva

Green is Good

Green are the hills, the valleys too
Out in the country where houses are few
How long will this be, always we hope
But what of the future can we cope?

Everyone must help to keep streams clean
Help all we can to have places fit to be seen
Is this a dream, will we all fail
Not if we try and fight tooth and nail.

Go out and plant lots of things
In the fresh air, we hear the bird sings
Pull up the weed put in new soil to feed
See your reward when up come the seed.

B Groves

The World's in a Crisis

The world's in a state
Such horror it does bring,
When children in their adolescence
The thought is worrying.

The jobs are poorly paid
Mortgages are high,
Bills paid frequently
But somehow I get by.

Shopping in the local town
Emptiness surrounds me
Plenty of shops, most bare
People haven't the money.

Corner shops used by few
Been slowly taken over,
Superstores selling in bulk
Cheaper prices, good rate of turnover.

Property dropped in value
Interest rates caused the trouble,
Only the minority
Able to avoid such struggle.

The world is in a crisis
Full of stress and strain,
But don't ever give up
Life never stays the same.

Sarah Whitehead

Winter

Winter
Beneath our feet,
Conceives
A bare retreat.
And in deep thought
Perceives
New leaves.

Winter
About our ears,
Does roar
Life from life sheers.
Wrecking raging
Rakes shore
Rakes raw.

Euanie Tippet

Without Rain

They sit on stones thirsting
the rain has failed to come,
roaming through the sunshine
a nightmare lingers on.
Children scorched while praying
waiting for specks to fall,
but prayers go unanswered
no God has answered their calls.

Everyone yearns the harvest
disease has come instead,
mosquitoes poison live bodies
parasites invade the dead.
Miles of drought and exposure
toiling to prevent all spoils,
there's no food in the granaries
no rain, no seeds, dried soil.

Rosemary Mundle

The Winds' Month

March is a shivery month. There's a snap to it.
It's the winds' month, and they do with it
as they please. The north wind snarls from
the Matlocks; people humped like question marks
skid on glass pavements and think longingly
of central heating. The south wind has business
elsewhere, but sometimes the south-west wind,
blustering, brings shell-breathing sounds of
mighty seas; breaks icicle fingers, and sets
blue violets nodding, watching the shivery lambs,
jumpy with new life.

Edith Spencer

Sunset

This year, last year, where has all the time gone,
Why are the months turning cold?
The last days of summer are dying away,
And I never knew I'd grown old.

Once I was younger than springtime, it seemed,
And the footsteps of time did run slow,
Now they all think I am older than death,
Where did those middle years go?

I remember my youth of laughter and fun
When I danced, it was not long ago.
Now the music has faded I ask once again,
Where did those dancing years go?

I picture myself on the day I was wed
In a gown that was whiter than snow,
My groom has departed and cannot now ask,
Where did our married years go?

My babes came along in the fullness of time,
Like flowers they started to grow,
I wonder if they ever pause to reflect,
Where did their childhood go?

Now the years quickly pass and life's nearly done,
I am bathed in the last sunset glow,
Perhaps in the future someone will ask
Where did that old lady go?

Ann Rutherford

The Fall of the Year

Ages ago, on this same field
Where I walk now, among the sheep,
A man looked upward, as I look,
Seeing the same cloud formations.
And he read there the same message
Of summer's decline into autumn,
Of the approaching equinox.
He noted the swallows' departure,
Drawn hence by invisible threads
To an unknown destination.
He worked the same land that I work
All day, and at dusk returning
Tired, to his primitive dwelling,
He knew that the winter was coming.
That the hard time was approaching.
He is the dust that the wind blows
Under my door in the morning.
He is the earth where, in the spring,
Young lambs will nibble the grasses.

Dorothy Steadman

A Prelude to Rhodes '93

The pound, pound, pound of people's feet,
The blank faced look of all in the street,
The sheeplike politeness of those I meet,
The monotonous sound of our daily beat.

Getaway!

Counting down from fifteen weeks,
How soon whittled down to fourteen sleeps.
Bloated on anticipation,
Ecstatic on expectation.

The planning and buying and borrowing
Provides entertainment whilst knowing
There'll be two strong weeks intensive drinking,
Capricious stunts and rowdy singing.

Several tapes crammed with serious tracks,
Practised mad dancing in local clubs when packed.
Improving physique and glancing through sales,
Impatient to inject into the night of females.

Recent clubland conquests augment my ego,
Ready for girls with ostentatious show.
Determined to win the challenge of best and worst,
To see of how many I can quench their thirst.

Returning experienced, satisfied and exhausted,
Plenty of stories to be retorted.
After the pranks, sex, dance, drinks, beatings,
Back to the North and its laboured conceiting.

Peter Jones

Eternal Truth

Through my window I look up and high
The same everywhere, vast blue sky.
All around, when my head I turn
As far as my eyes can discern.

A speck in the distance, now I see
It's a bird, a creature like me.
In this universe of creation
Like an atom in the mighty ocean.

Look now, and, something has changed
Unseen artist has rearranged,
Beauty of the universe dazzling new
Change is the life, as known by the few.

Nucleus at the centre, plasma around
With a membrane all particles bound;
Stars, planets, the earth and sky
Who kept them there, I wonder why.

Some said God, others called Nature
Surely, beyond any wise preacher;
May not you feel, may not you see
It's the same, in you and me.

'What's the matter, where is the mind
We aren't the same, different in kind'
Say not so; as only in name,
Statues are many, clay is the same . . .

Specks in the universe, whatever we call
Absolute truth makes them small;
Part of the whole aren't we all?
What does it matter, we each other call.

Anand Deshpande

The Star

A bright star moved quickly
As fast as it can be,
And down into the atmosphere
It seemed so close - so near.

And as it dropped it flew
For a while it seemed to you,
That it was going to land
How you could not expand.

The quiff it disappeared
Like when it first appeared,
Something inside died
Why so cruel you cried.

But deep into another time
The message on the line,
Is that it's natural
For stars to fall.

Mike Vuicasinovic

Life

In youth, our world we explore
Like wind and waves, that crash on shore,
Water cuts, like edge of knife
A swirling, roaring pulse of life,
Simple pleasures like glowing stars
Chiming bells and dinky cars.

In prime, we work amidst life's dreams
Notions, of fantasy it seems,
Enraptured by first tugs of love
Soaring high, through clouds above,
We set the stage, for life's next chapter
But what is real, and who's the actor?

Caught off guard, our time is nigh
Reversal, to an age gone by,
Cognitive functions, prone to decay
Like supple flesh, that ebbs away,
Death, he comes to make his mark
Like a flickering fire made dark.

Mary Carradice

Manchester Bus Station

The man stands by the bus,
His children sit by the window,
The man makes funny faces,
The children laugh
Daddy! Daddy!

He holds up a white peppermint cream
Like the Holy Grail.
His wife sits with stony eyes:
As the bus moves
The children are hers.
In the man's heart a tear stirs.
Destination, destination.

Maureen Weldon

Life in the North West When I was a Lad

It were tuppence a bus ride when I were a lad
But things have change since, and I'm glad
From pebbled roads and pebbled streets
To tar mac and flags lay nice and neat.

When I was a lad my Ma used to say,
'Mark my words it will all change one day.'
He by eck she was not far wrong,
For it did change and it didn't take long.

They gave a whole new look to the North West
Pulled down old buildings and put up the best,
New precincts, shops, houses too
And lots of new things for people to do.

When I were a lad if you walked down our street
I'd have holes in my clothes and nought on my feet,
You don't see out like that these days
For now people have changed their ways.

Changed for the best I'm glad to say
Well people have that live round our way,
I'd really hate to have to move away
The North West is where I wanna stay.

Linda Smith

The Four Swans

I saw four swans afloating along the Dukinfield Ship Canal.
They pleased my heart, and my Soul, and by gum, they didn't half
look well.
Now two of the four, were as white as snow, and the other two,
not quite,
But, even so, together, they made such a pretty sight.
One of the four, kept putting its head to the shore,
Presumably, looking for food, whilst I, on the side, could
only look on with pride,
and think, what a beautiful creation you are.
One thing I know, and that's for sure, the next time I'm out walking,
I'll visit again, that ship canal, and listen, to those swans, talking.

The Wanderer

16

Battle of the Seasons

It is raining nearly every day
The summer thinks winter is here to stay,
Will the sun get a look-in, to shine and to beckon
Not very likely the winter does reckon.
The spring is a time of renewal from death
But it's all mixed up since the greenhouse effect,
Things bloom and die at peculiar times
When will the rain stop and dry all the plains.
In autumn an Indian summer is had
The leaves flow around as we're scantily clad,
The seasons are changing year by year
Affected by pollution in the atmosphere.
The dates should be changed so we will know
When to expect rain, wind, sun or snow.

Marcia J Galley

Our Lovely Little Village

Oh, how lovely was the village
Where I was born, and bred
Where we were always surrounded
By Mother Nature down the years.
We had favourite walks
Where we used to pick wild flowers,
We enjoyed the solicitude and happiness
That came through being content,
And peace of mind.
But now the greedy developers
Have come to build houses,
And little estates
On our precious pastures
Where we used to play.
And now its noisy with big waggons
Tractors, cars, and vans
From morn 'til night
And through the night.
Thirty miles is the limit, past my home
But more often it is at forty mile they go,
It's become more like a town
There is noise, everywhere we go.
But thank God there are a few places
That reminds me of Tarleton my birth place,
That once was a lovely village.

M A Topping

18

Geese in Winter

All round the frosted pond they stand
Like white torches
In the dim midwinter light,
Waiting, waiting.
Waiting for what?
The return of warmth to snowy backs?
The dance of sun on pond?
No.
Waiting for the warmth of a bright kitchen,
With heat wafting from an oven,
And pans steaming on a stove,
And all round a table
Festoons of smiles and shining eyes, waiting.

Colin Wingfield

Autumn

Dry discarded leaves,
Drifting gently down,
Each one like a year of life,
Their season having past,
Sweet green youth has flown away,
And ageing winter's closing fast.

Carole Sexton

Memories

'E bye gum I'm champion
Yorkshire through and through,
Bred and born in Yorkshire
An right proud of it too.

Bread and jam
And Yorkshire pud
Tripe and onions too,
Black pud and bread and drip
Just to name a few.

Pit boots and snap tins
Clogs and shawl,
Cloth cap and muffler
Says it all.

A pint at the pub
Packet of fags,
A night at the dogs
With a few of the lads.

A bag of chips
On your way home from the flicks
And you didn't have to queue,
A glowing fire when you got home
And mam waiting with a brew.

Mildred Fardell

Waterstone

Rain rusted bracken
scattered through the gorse spines
pinning soil to fell side,
choking down to beck side
feeding off the razor crag.

Stooping at the water's edge
half fallen to its golden bed
guided by a magpie eye,
I push with my meniscus glove
rain chasing, through the kissing cold
clearer than air.

Hauling home a coloured stone
a red poppy on a field of corn
fast fading in my drying palm,
like drowning wild flowers
in a vase.

Russell Gee

The Maypole

We've gathered together, it's a happy scene,
Today we're choosing our own May Queen,
With lace on her head, and a curtain train,
The likes, you'll never see again
The hoop, covered with flowers of every hue,
All made with paper, and stuck on with glue.
The boys all jeering, and calling out names,
They'd really love to be a part of our games.
At last we're all ready, and off we go,
From door to door with our show.
The people come from near and far
Pennies, jingling in our jar,
We'll all have a party, with jelly and cream
The boys will be welcome to this happy scene.
We dance round the Maypole, singing the May dance song.
Even the grown ups are part of this throng.
As the evening shadows begin to appear
We pack things away, until May next year.

E Powell

Seasons

A sense of fear as the fog descends
Enveloping you in a blanket of gloom,
It smothers, it chokes, and it hides,
Your worst nightmares within.

With it comes the dark,
The sudden descent of night,
You're left blind, unable to see,
Frantic, and it's cold.

The wind snaps at you
With a thousand teeth,
Tearing the flesh from your bones
Shivering as it penetrates your soul
And passes through.

An explosion of light,
The sun appears on the horizon,
You stand transfixed
As a hare caught in the glare of a headlight.

Then the warmth,
The snugness and security of a mother's embrace
The memory of pain and despair slowly fading.

The colours of happiness leap out at you
Yellow gold of buttercup, emerald green of grass,
The enchanting drone of insects
The comforting whisper of a breeze.

It's summer in my life
The nightmare and loneliness of winter passed
Enjoy it while you can
As around the corner, who knows?

Craig Parker

The Warning

The mist came down over the big wood,
As I knew it always would.
Meaning it was a sign of rain
Signs of the countryside were hard to explain.

Birds of the countryside would leave the scene,
Warning of a wind so strong and supreme,
When it came with lashing rain,
Stopping the birds coming back again.

The lowing of cattle late at night.
The cattle warning the night was, too bright.
Then by the following dawning,
People should have heeded the cattle's warning.

Snow came and lay thick all around.
Making it difficult for things to be found,
Snow made it hard for people to proceed.
The cattle's warning was not taken to heed.

When the snow, wind and rain, had gone away,
The birds returned, and the cattle did lay.
So in future, take heed of the warning sound,
The birds and cattle send abound.

Kenneth Matthews

Hurricane 1987

Began the quiet morning,
    With breeze soft and gentle,
A wind that blew stronger all through the day long,
    As fell the grey twilight
    To bring dusk and darkness,
Give birth to the gale that would drown the birds song.

The sea became restless
    With white foaming horses,
And all through the land the trees waited their doom,
    Like so many soldiers,
    No strength in their numbers,
The old and the young in the gathering gloom.

Their age did not matter,
    The wind showed no mercy,
That night when those millions of trees were laid low,
    The oaks from whose branches
    Came wood for the Navy,
All felled to the ground by the mightiest blow.

'Tis now but a memory,
    As years bring their comfort,
And stumps lie all covered with grass and with flowers,
    The trunks still lie scattered,
    For folk to remember
The night the wind struck in the terrible hours.

The birds have returned and
    The sheep are now grazing,
Where wind tore great swaythes through the woods and the leas,
    Still stands the small cottage,
    The church in the meadow,
And leaves grow again on the newly-born trees.

P G Elgar

Song of Silence

When the Downs stretch out before you
And the sky is high and wide,
Where the silhouettes of shrub and tree
Span out the countryside.
When the roads are far behind you
And the birds are on the wing,
You can linger there - in the fresh sweet air
To hear the silence sing.

When the night has spread a jewelled net
Of stars - across the sky,
And the blood red sun has slipped away
Like a warrior - to die.
When the cares of day - are swept away
In the peace that night can bring,
You can stand there - in the cool sweet air
To hear the silence sing.

Have you heard the Song of Silence?
As you wander through the Downs,
And gaze at hills that flaunt their trees
Atop - like stately crowns.
Just stand awhile and listen
To the whisper of the grass,
The movement of a branch or leaf
As breezes gently pass -
How strange and lovely this can be
When the flutter of a wing,
Can set the words to music
And make the silence sing.

Dorothy Carter

Hazel and Brown

The time it was the fall,
The leaves were hazel and brown,
Falling from the trees,
Like falling to your knees,
When you strive to reach the dreams
Of the one you love.

The fate of the leaves, however,
Is to fall only to the ground,
Like so many before,
And many after, drowned,
Then to be whisked away,
When all was but forgotten,
By a warm and carrying breeze,
Like whispy ghosts of cotton.

Like the nature's butterfly,
Caressing the flowers it lands,
Taken on their journey,
And onto warmer sands,
Through the icy bitterness of winter,
To the hopeful blossoming of spring,
And on to the warm romance of summer,
And all the hope it brings.

Then to return to the fall,
Where they are once again,
Leaves but Hazel and Brown,
Who dreamt away their pain.

Richard Daniels

Spring Extravaganza

(Being a Monday morning classroom reverie on a perfect
spring day of a Surrey Schoolmaster still alive to
impulses, visibly stirring in the young committed to his charge.)

Why are you dreaming, where are your thoughts?
Why can't you concentrate, quite out of sorts?
Little boys chatter and scribble and mess
And you let 'em do it, couldn't care less!
- I couldn't care less, for what do I see
On the moving screen of memory? -

Pale gold sunshine filtering
Through those Surrey copses where nightingales sing;
Broad sweeps of bluebells' shimmering mist,
And the blush a wild apple sunbeam kissed;
Masses of mayflowers' cream-speckled foam,
And the billowing chestnut tree's candlelit dome;
Birdsong and flowers, fragile and fair,
And the thrust and the lunge of life everywhere.

The thrust and the lunge in the teeming wood,
The surge of the sap in the bursting bud,
The rapture of birdsong, virile and proud,
The joy of creation shouting aloud!
And life in abundance, responsive and glad,
Through the veins blithely racing like mad,
The worship of Maia, or Freya, or Pan,
The primal impulses of earliest man!

Oh, to be back in the heart of the wood,
Senses a-tingle with joy in the blood,
Eager, responsive, bursting to share
In the teeming abundance of all the life there!
What am I doing, with shuttered-down mind,
Curbing these children, blind leading the blind?
Oh, let the bell ring, and far away fling
Pens textbooks and paper, and let us take wing
With zest and abandon, our tributes to bring
To this ravishing, exquisite, wanton, wild spring!

Alwyn Trubshaw

Longing

Clouds high over distant downs
Blown by wind like a maiden's hair,
Which clings and tickles upon moist brow
Or stream that moves the soft green weed;
And waves as in a wheatfield sea
Each movement suggest the tresses flow.

I'm part of nature's current now
Courage wanes with the water flow,
My will is stilled by sylphlike music
Spirit free as waters eddy,
Now hold me close my love
So we may caress 'til morning comes.

A W E Davis

Swifts and Swallows in Spring

Darting, diving,
Searching, striving,
Scooping, swooping,
Loop the looping.

Such a graceful display
On a fine spring day;
I stand and stare
In the mild, soft air
And admire the skill
Of each streamlined quill.
So much power!
So much speed!
And all for greed;
Such great acrobats!
Just to feed on gnats.

Jane Wilson

From Where the Window Sits

(For Jock.)

From where the window sits
               (I on the lap),
The broadening world scopes the view.
And it is no pretty thing -
Not picturesque as the gardens would purport.
No, houses are a solemn sight:
Packed in solemn rows: bushes, flowers,
Plants touched up like a worn face
Benevolently lying.

All I see in this are temporal things.
Each gate turns inward;
Each pathway door-bound;
Each lopping tree anchored
To a thought of he who brought it.
Cynically, he thought: *Let it grow tall*
And grand before I die.

Samuel Slatter

33

Untitled

They're taking us down you know,
It only takes one final blow
To go.

The landscape looks urban and dreary,
My branches are leaden and weary
Not cheery.

The planners said it was all right you see,
My owner just rubbed his hands with glee
He's free.

Every tree worth its weight in gold,
Who dares make that last is so bold
To be told.

That urbanization must happen you see,
Living trees are not allowed to be free
Like me.

Anne Morris

34

Ode to a Weed

I'm on nodding terms with the Hollyhock,
I admire her stately pose.
And my next-door neighbour on my right
Is a Floribunda rose.
She showers me with fragrance
When her petals start to fall.
But the bindweed, that entwined weed -
        Climb up and over all!

Delphiniums bid me time of day
Standing tall above the ground.
While the Foxgloves flare their nostrils
And look warily around:
At a haze of blue Forget-me knots
In clumps about their feet.
But the bindweed, that unkind weed -
        Nobody wants to greet!

If I lift my head when soft winds blow,
And I do when I get the chance.
I can see the Canterbury Bells
Swaying as in a trance.
Kissing-cousins to Campanula,
In pastel blue and white.
Like the bindweed, unrefined weed -
        Never out of sight!

The arrival of the Chrysanthemums
All frilled in the autumn breeze,
Add a final touch of splendour
As sweet summer takes her leave.
The humblest of nature's flowers,
My time is nearly up.
Not the bindweed, much maligned weed.
        I'm the creeping Buttercup.

Iris Allingham

We Need to Know

We need to know you really do care
For the big things and little things in life we share.
The birds that fly so free
Each and every single tree,
The flowers that grow and blossom so bright
The sun in the morning and the moon at night.

We need to know you really do care
For all the animals that have been left so rare.
Thunder and lightning wind and rain
Every bus, car, lorry and train,
Buildings some very new and some very old
The weather in the winter that is so cold.

We need to know you really do care
About how we breathe is it really clean air,
For the young and old and in-betweens too
For the life we all have that goes for me and you,
For the next generation that take over what we leave
Hoping there is something left for them to retrieve.

We need to know you really do care
About the state this world is in and the Ozone layer.
For the grass that's really green
Will it stay that way is yet to be seen,
For the material things that give us a lift
Do you really care that each and everything in life is a gift.

Carol Scoular

One Small Wish

If someone granted me a wish I think that it might be
A change in viewpoint for mankind, and less of me, me, me.
But changing this would be to change the chemistry of man,
For he's behaved precisely thus since every life began.

It's only now that we perceive the error of our ways -
Was it innocence or ignorance that numbered our last days?
When once we took but ne'er replaced, the land seemed rich and full
We've taken all, discarded most and left a broken hull.

For once we foresaw riches and a dream of growth and wealth
We built on our inheritance and disregarded health.
Too late we learnt that our respect for life could save our plight
As dust-caked smoke-blacked chimneys belch filth into the night.

But now we see - too late we cry - that money can't solve all
For Earth's own fate is on the scales, and man must take a fall.
For we can't buy an ozone patch or acres of new trees,
We own no fault but guilty yet we fonder on our knees.

So what remains for us to do, but writhe and twist in guilt?
For all must help and yet it seems the milk's already spilt.
We give up using aerosols and rush to go lead-free
To ease our troubled consciences and hope to let things be.

There is a corner somewhere still where far from suits and cars
The smoky city bustle ends and twilight shines with stars.
Where man can hope and dream and take a breath of scent-filled air
And lie and laugh in breeze-swept grass without the slightest care . .
.

Hayley Moffatt

Walking in the Woods

Trees beckoning
Fresh air anticipating,
Leisurely walking
Leaves crackling.
Children scrambling
Voices echoing,
Blackberry picking
Dogs barking.
Paths weaving
Sun dappling,
Clouds rolling
Rain dripping.
Wellies squelching
Hill slipping,
Home coming
Tea sipping.

Sue Barker

Ornamental Garden

Resilient weed appears in the sunlight
Bright and fresh before the flowers,
Cultivated colours, strong yet impure
Moulded and created, not by nature,
But by a continued filtering of ideas,
Until the perfect bloom is found.
Still invaded by the unwanted weed;
Extroverts amid the fragile design.

Nature's intruder will always return.
No restraining hand can remove it.
Always fighting for the right to survive.
Now beneath their colourful purity
Hides a vengeful, destructive force.
No lenience with Man's fickle flowers,
So they thrive to control, then destroy.

Melanie Russell

The War in Yugoslavia

What is being done for the Yugoslavs?
Where people are killed, raped, or starved.
Their homes blown to pieces, right to the ground
People's lives destroyed, with a shelling sound.
What is the world doing - just gone mad?
Just watching TV and feeling sad.
Aid is sent, for the sick and wounded,
But no retaliation of aggression, can be founded.
When is this war going to stop?
When the politicians, just talk shop!
The time is now, for forces to go in,
To stop all atrocities of death and sin.
The people of Yugoslavia must be saved,
From the fear of going to an early grave.
Don't let them destroy the human race
It's the most precious gift on this Earth's face.

Paul Hough

Autumn

Neglect that one cannot restore
Nor add a gentler air to balm,
The rendings and the cutting edge of wind
The supple leaf to harm.

Erect against the littered rock
The rigid heather pinks with cold,
And scentless in their stubbled mass
Speak gently to the passing old.

Songs that once possessed the air
Have fled in haste to hide their fears,
Yellow to its sun-lit heart the oak
Shines forth to shed dry tears.

Painted all, but so short lived
For well we know the best is brief,
As autumn turns upon the bough
To scattered shreds and pale relief.

Clive Harvey

After the Hurricane

The leaves - they will not turn this year
To colours red and brown
Of seven oaks, only the one
Is left to grace our town.
A hundred years of birch and pine,
Of chestnut, beech and fir,
Stretch out their torn and mangled limbs
Like corpses in the air.
I know, Lord, that you guide our ways,
You saved our lives, you care.
And there will be another spring
To clothe our gardens bare.
But you who sent the lights that burned,
The mighty winds that blew,
Give us the strength to build again
The Edens that we knew.

Marion Shephard

The Wind

She moans like one in sickness
    And screams as if in pain,
She rages like a torrent
    And lashes at the rain
The seas are tossed in turmoil
    And ships like matchwood sway,
Her power has never been surpassed
    In strength she rules the waves.

Destruction can be rampant
    At times when she's around
There's no-one that can tame her.
    Or brake, or keep her bound.
For freedom she possesses
    To rise, and fall at will.
No man can ever hold her,
    Destroy, or keep her still.

E Walsh

Woodland

Singing are the birds in the trees
Buzzing are the wasps and the bees.
Trees are swaying in the breeze so light,
And the glaring sun is shining bright.
Leaves are falling from waving branches,
And the clouds are floating in wonderful trances.
Bluetits are tweeting and soaring around,
And robins are pecking worms from the ground.
Flowers are dancing, squirrels are prancing.
Rabbits are leaping, hedgehogs are sleeping.
Mice are scattering, grey rats are nattering.
Wolves are heard howling, foxes are growling
But moths are quietly flying along.
Cherries are shining in a smooth red lining,
And badgers are dining.
Sparrows are chirping in the windy trees.
Sunset appears, now not so bright,
The sky turns black, it's night.
Now there's nothing, all is silent,
No more fox growls which had once been violent.
The moon is full, birds hide in their nests.
And the woodland waits for morning,
And lies still, in rest.

Marie Reynolds

Clouds

Clouds are not loud
They are silent and deep,
And pass by your window
While you are asleep.

What would they say
If they told all they see,
I'm sure all the stories
Would shock you and me.

They travel the world
Not saying a word,
As swift as the breeze
And as light as a bird.

Wouldn't it be lovely
To be free from all worry,
Free as a cloud
And in no sort of hurry.

E Casey

Viva Los Canarios

Our lazy Summer holidays are over once again
We lapped up all the sun there was, and didn't see much rain.
The days were long, the company fun
We were sorry to leave when our time was done.

The walk from the sands to our hotel
Was so pleasant . . . except for that awful smell!
A stall at the entrance to the beach would do well
Selling pegs - ten pesetas each!

At night we slept sound as a rock
But not 'til after two o'clock
When all was silent, calm and sweet
After the discos insistent beat.

Good food in the dining room, a holiday's requisite
One shouldn't have to peer and say, 'Dear God, whatever is it?'
Rice pudding, and pink blancmange, a gourmet treat before
Have a feeling if I served it now, I'd be smartly shown the door!

Flies and wasps, mosquito bites beneath a silvery moon
The Manufacturers of TCP must make a blooming fortune.
Calluses and blisters from hiking into town
Ensure the Band-Aid factories never will close down.

And yet, in spite of all the moans, discomfort woes and pain
Come next year we'll book our hols . . . and off we'll go again!

Margaret Hansford

Godfather Tree

See my leaves that fall in Autumn
Never see my tears,
See my splendour lost in winter
Never lost my pride.
See my new self grow in Springtime
With new confidence,
See the fruit I bear in summer
Alas, I bear the brunt.
Mankind's had enough of me
They're not ashamed to say,
But I've been here for centuries
Not just a passing day.
Evil's reigned and peasants fought
Won battles on the green,
From times forgot to present day
My branches shade the scene.
The wildlife here that whistles sweet
And dance so happily,
The cherubs falling from the clouds
Are real, not fantasy.
Such beauty here, such innocence
Watch children as they play,
See crystal tears fall as they weep
When told it ends today.
Then future generations hear
Because they cannot see,
The pillar of four seasons gone
Goodbye Godfather Tree.

Steve Taylor

Light

In between the houses
I can see gaps of light
Another world
Hills, trees, the river
Of life still flows.

In between the houses
More houses, more streets,
Factories, roads.
No light but a
Sheen of grey.

In between the fields
I can see a house,
And a tree
A river flowing
And sitting by it,
Me.

Chris Wattam

A Cotswold Homecoming

We've been amid the granite
of the mighty peaks up north;
We've sailed the Tay and traversed
the bridge across the Forth.
We've watched the gannets plunging
from the Mull of Old Kintyre
and seen Loch Ranza glowing
in the summer sunset fire.

Now we have left the Vikings.
We travel the Saxon land
where hills are low and kindly . . .
Around us on every hand
the ancient fields and hedgerows,
the soaring village spires
proclaim the common heritage
of these, our Mercian shires.

Further south in Cotswold,
once home of Offa's throne,
Churches and walls and houses
of light-refracting stone,
wide horizons, native trees,
oaks beech and churchyard yew
all join to bid us welcome
as Home comes into view.

What's happened since we went away?
And did the milkman call today?

Alfred Leeding

49

Charlie's Home

A land
That killed a king,
Then housed another.
A refuge from the wrath
Of his Germanic Mother,
That tied the knot
With Flora his brother.
That hid the soul
Of his one true lover,
That fell to the sea
Where the tide ran high,
In autumnal yellow
Against a slated sky.

Justin Elliott

A Tunnel

The between time
from Warwickshire to Leicestershire,
A Tunnel, a damp drizzle of forty minutes.

The between time
from Northamptonshire to Warwickshire,
A Tunnel, a dark decapitating ten minutes.

The between time
from youth to marriage,
A Tunnel of accidents, sex, fertile, trouble.

The between time
from love to hate,
A Tunnel of duvets.

The between time
from life to death,
forget the tunnels,
Enjoy life.

Jean E Bradley

The Long Road

As we breathe in and let out a sigh
We realise that time is passing us by,
We plod through life with our various loads
Treading the long and wearying roads,
We always seem to take the long way round
In search of answers to be found.
No maps are given to help our search
So sometimes on the fence we perch,
While we decide which way to go
Indecision making the going slow,
No help at hand as we go it alone
Tripping over the obstacles that we are prone,
But just as we turn a bend
We find that this road has no end,
By now though our steps are getting stronger
Our stance is upright our strides are longer,
Now we are feeling more sure
And can face what life has in store.

Anita Aplin

Sandycroft Road Churchdown

Rambling the green lane memories of my smallest years,
I recall a lake so vast that the whole summer was swallowed
By its perch-laden waters.
So large that our lead-weight casting was
But a dragonfly settling on its hide.
So deep that the morning they sent electricity through its depths
It took all day, and more, to net the stunned fish.
So mighty that even after being filled,
Seven sad and long years passed before the new earth was still.

Wandering the gravel track memories of my early years,
I recall a broken cottage sitting haunted
At the dark end of our road.
Her walls being engulfed by the slow green and yellow fingers
Of her wild and beautiful garden.
So scary, only a dare could ever drive us inside to meet with
Scurrying spectral mice, the drip of unholy water, woodworm and
rust.
Yet the men that tore her down and levelled
Her grounds seemed not scared in the least.

Prowling the concrete road memories of my younger years
I recall a scrapyard that, to small eyes, stretched shining
Diamond-like above and beyond all the horizon.
Staircases of bright jalopies, saloons and estates,
And grass growing through broken windscreens.
Though a muscled boxer that growled within made it a rare day
That we climbed the fence into this wonderland.
Now the staircases have been replaced with foundations for the
future.

Loitering upon the asphalt memories of my teenage years
I recall tripods upon the road and chalk marks
Upon old creosoted fences.
Where there was a home and a real garden with
Room for dogs and hens to laze in the sun,
There would soon be eight houses
With space not even for shadows between.
Dump trucks and pneumatic drills, bricks red and bright, open plan.
And saddest of all, of course, goodbyes.

Derek Rutherford

Home

In my well built house
Do I take my rest,
And there in the eve'
I eat of the best.
Tho' nowise a King am I
Elsewhere on Earth,
Most noble of Lords am I
By my own hearth.

Barry Sowter

Herefordshire and Worcestershire

Sunshine and shadows
Orchards of delight,
Glistening apples and plump plums,
Tractors amble across rich soil.
Shire horses and steam engines gather the crowds,
Castles and monuments are to be found
Ancient buildings in market towns
Hops smell sweetly in the September air.
It's a land of mellow fruitfulness,
Edging the Welsh borders
A blossoming county of England.

G Davis

Trees

Do you ever stop to look at trees,
As the wind dips their boughs and rustles the leaves.
Leafy oaks and poplars tall.
A willow peeps over a garden wall.
The chestnut with candles all aglow
Conkers in the autumn grow.
A fir tree with its pine needles so very green
At Christmastime is a pretty scene.
Beech, ash, and sycamore are a few
Nature lovers do adore.
So when you walk down a country lane,
You will find it has not been in vain.
Look around and you will see
There's nothing more elegant than a tree.

Freda Nicholson

Time Past

Castle Kings Knights of old
Where dragons once boldly stroll,
Where pasture green and forests grown
and an everlasting dew.
Where rain once hit upon the ground
A rainbow shines all around, and once
the rain has passed away - it turns into a
Lovely day.

J Summerfield

Life Forces

Pure-flowing stream -
        ever bright,
        continually renewed.
Every moment as I gaze
you show me that this instant, now,
        can be
a fresh beginning.

Scented bloom -
        unforced, inevitable,
        exquisite dose of beauty. Joyful acclamation
From pinpoint seed
        to fragrant drop of joy;
        You will not fail.
You waken me to see what Paradise
        is very Life itself.
You urge me seek a deeper comfort still.

Potent creative power,
        golden splendour of the sun,
        cold glories of a snowy-dawn,
        dewy-diamon'd web,
eternal signs that Earth is good.

And from the ocean, earth and skies
        I gaze at happy smiling eyes;
        I'm bid to strive, to use my power,
        inexpressible, within,
to cause that other one to see, in waves of Love,
        the reason why I'm fashioned me.

Miracle of storm, and sunny quietness,
Miracle of mind, of body,
     of moods, and weaknesses profound,
     calmed through the sweetness of sleep;
But in the stormy traffic of our days,
     myopic schemes, rash words and bodies over-stretched
Miracle of consolation - two caring souls, they solve
     their fear and panic,
     they soothe their troubled minds,
     touching together in their mutual warmth.

David Bayley

The Sun

All was dim, just the remnants of a mist,
Pierced faintly by the blueness of the moon,
Then it came, like the cool of a breeze.
A deep orange, ambered, glow rose,
Touching every object, flickering as it toyed
With the boughs and branches in the trees.
It danced around the pound, crystalised its surface,
Lighting it up with a million heavenly stars.
Skipped up and down the roof tops,
Turning windows bright light, golden
The houses and the cars.
All was silent, just the sound of wind,
Singing sweet duets softly with the mist -
Breathing life all around (I see)
Two pure white swans, stretch their wings pull upright
Before they leave the ground
I trace their flight, I notice the ambered glow,
Turns life's blood red,
Behind their mawkish silhouettes,
Now out of sight, I cast a sigh in wonderment,
As my emotions set me thinking of splendours romantic concepts.
In the time that has passed,
My sensations overflow, to see this beauty.
Oh revered inspiring fun,
To hope every day will start like this, for me it surely will
For all I have is to remember to look up to the sun.

Glen Wills

Queen of the Midlands

There is so much beauty in this world.
So much to do and see,
Here in the heart of the Midlands
Is a lovely place to be.
Nottingham is my home town
Of Robin Hood renown,
Famous for many things
Lace, the University, with its statue of Jessie Boot.
Walking in Wollaton Park, or by the River Trent.
Here is where my heart sings
We have Raleigh bicycles, John Player and Son.
Also our wonderful castle
Where legend has it, Maid Marian's hand was won
When it comes to fun things,
Goose Fair is hard to beat
The famous Trip to Jerusalem is a very old pub indeed.
There in the magic hours, friends and lovers meet
Here is where my roots are, its treasures many to see.
Nottingham, Queen of the Midlands
Is the favourite place for me.

Olive Partridge

Woodland Fields

It's beautiful in God's garden,
Where nature is at peace,
The clouds roll on and on,
And think of me not least.

The sun eternally shines
The air is fresh and clean.
The pace is slow and calm,
What can the human race mean.

There is nothing worth for rushing,
There is nothing that compares to this,
What pace of life we lead,
Look at all we miss.

Let me grab this tranquil moment
And never let it part,
So when I'm rushing around,
I can recreate it in my heart.

T England

Autumn Morning Bus Ride

Long grey faces, long grey faces,
autumn morn.
Chimneys smoking, smoking chimneys,
early dawn.
Heads in shoulders hunched 'gainst coldness.
Shapeless mass of human form.
Cold grey day.

No one laughing, no one smiling,
faces grim
Potted houses, houses potted,
gardens trim.
Have we lost the heart required
to love our fellow men.
Are we all so very tired to want
to start again.
Cold grey day.

No one speaking, no one looking,
passing life with sightless eyes.
Never caring, never sharing other's troubles
leaden skies.
Helping hands are not extended at
this hour of the day.
Huddled forms of shrunken people,
hurry on their secret way.
Cold grey day.

Comes the evening, workday over,
scowl no more.
To seek solace in one's family,
nothing's sure.
Why should others ever see us if
we live in such a way.
Should we change or pass forever
in this tragic lonely way
Cold grey day.

Can't we lift our eyes to others.
Can't we know just what to say.
Hold your own trial, before condemning
just what others never say.
Clear your heart of all its greyness,
just to find a deeper grey.
Cold grey day . . .

R Shufflebotham

In Appreciation of Daventry Wildlife Country Park

Oh country park, a place to be,
For me to find tranquillity,
From fresh spring buds, until autumn fall,
Each day new visions to recall
Foliage changing throughout the year,
Among wild flowers extremely rare
Primrose, snowdrop and violets amass,
Nestling in the fresh spring grass,
Blossoming hawthorn, rowan, cherries,
All too soon will change to berries
There to give us winter cheer,
And feed the birds when all is bare.

A children's playground, with lots to do,
A waterside picnic area too,
Where swans and geese wait to see,
Just who is calling in for tea?
A lovely sheltered hide sublime,
To just relax, and take some time
To watch the water birds at play,
Tempted to sit and watch all day,
A bird I see but can't recall,
I consult the chart upon the wall.

The water mirror's fine reflection,
Coloured pictures, such perfection,
Squirrels leap from tree to tree,
Showing off for all to see.
Spotted woodpeckers hammer away,
Whilst cuckoos call throughout the day,
Such a variety of lovely trees,
Fields, ponds, bogs, all there to please.
Dragonfly, butterfly, birds and bees,
Rodents, frogs and water fleas.

Iris add colour to the bogs,
Insects scamper in the logs
Honeysuckle, yellow broom,
Pink wild roses, sweet perfume,
Country park a joy to me,
With so many natural things to see,
In my declining days of leisure,
Thank you for giving me such pleasure.

Harold Cox

Old England

How great is dear Old England,
Where all the oak trees stand.
It's been that way for a thousand years
Growing proud, and tall, and grand.

It's spread those great wide branches,
Adorned itself in green.
And made its place a haven,
Of which, others only dream.

Its outlook is so wonderful
Next, the rolling countryside.
Where lovely birds, squirrels and rabbits,
Often visit there, to hide.

They playfully are bounding
Around the home, they've found.
With loud squeaks, spills and chatter,
Thinking, they are safe and sound.

But tales come thro' the pretty stream
Of total devastation.
Of men, who wish to change this place,
In the name of privatisation.

So, blind panic sets the heart aflame,
For there'll be nowhere deer, to hide.
Now this place is full of cunning fox,
And those *billboards*, go up, beside.

So, you'll all have to find a new home,
For they'll cut the Great Oak, down.
That sight you saw those years ago,
Will never more - be found.

Sue Williams

Dream Ticket

In a lottery of dream destinations
the winning ticket's right before your eyes.

Instead of catching cabs or meeting at the station,
you'll be leaping over wooden stiles.

At one with nature in an old fashioned way
following ancient paths with historic meanings.

No cities with associated troubles, so you may
discover a way of life that is peaceful and green.

By now you should know where your dream ticket takes you
somewhere beautiful, simple and old.

Without worry it is clear you can now set off
to the ever engaging Cotswolds.

James Davis

England

England is the place for me,
Nowhere else I'd rather be,
I've travelled far and travelled wide,
But none compare with her outside,
Her charm and beauty cast a spell,
Around all those who nearby dwell,
While her summer smile so soft and warm,
Can chase away the darkest storm,
I'm content - no more to stray,
Here beside her I will stay,
And when it's time for me to die,
Locked in her bosom I will lie.

Alison Jager

Past and Present - Yet What's the Future?

When no bricks or mortar were lay down
We then had a small but beautiful town.
There was a simple part of the countryside
With little meadows and apple trees
And our proud river running slow and free.

This town has now changed with a city overflow,
This town may be a lot bigger
But we true yokels have nowhere left to go.
Another row of hedges get cut down,
Making way for this ever expanding town.

Metal and concrete, tarmac and clay,
Now boldly take the place of
Where a farmer once proudly cut down hay.
And where trees stood so proud
Estates have taken up their ground.

Nature has now left with the foxes that played
No more lovely pictures will be portrayed.
Long roads creep in slowly turning to cross
Putting all their riders into a loss.
That's what it was then,
And that's just a little of what's now.
No one can say what's in the future, no way no how.

Phillip Kesterton

Oxford Street Daze (Days)

Long legged damsels,
Showing no signs of distress,
Only of opulence
In varying degrees of undress.

The rustling - the bustling,
The sense of senseless urgency,
Suspended in the frantic air
No evidence of an emergency.

The raucous hawk
Of a manic trader,
In contrast - in rags
To a lady - he bade her.

'Look 'ere luv
I got what you need,'
She tossed her head
Paying him no further heed.

People of all kinds
Shapes, sizes, colours and sounds,
Note the city gent, resplendent,
Secure in his pin stripe gown.

Tourists galore,
Emitting bewildered looks,
Abundant cameras
And hastily procured books.

Beatific faces
Adorned with delirious delight,
Oxford Street daze
I ponder what of the night.

Tony Wilson

The Age of the Nuclear Family

Fred and Sue live in a concrete house near Milton Keynes
Where the concrete cows dream concrete dreams,
They drive down concrete roads to concrete shops
And buy frozen food like concrete blocks.
But the local pub has old oak beams
And the kids like to play on the fruit machines,
While Madonna sings on the video screen
In the age of the nuclear family.

He drives a turbo car and there's a turbo mower
She's got a turbo fridge and there's a turbo drier,
There's Zanussi, Sony, Sansui and Saisho
And the kids watch an old war film on the JVC video.
But now Fred's struggling with the spreadsheets on the Amstrad PC
He's juggling with figures he can't get to agree,
The bills are so high they're using so much energy
Living in the age of the nuclear family.

Nuclear power's alright by Fred
He likes the remote control that works on infrared,
The electric toothbrush and the ultraviolet sun-bed
Has made his body brown.
But it's made him weak in the head
Cos he doesn't know where the waste goes,
Never even heard of Elstow
And nuclear-free and CND.
Are issues with which he could hardly agree
But don't blame Fred he's just one of many,
Living in the age of the nuclear family.

Dan Evans

Untitled

I have loved Gloucestershire above all other places
the very thought of her is inbred in my bones.
And though I left her in the middle years
Wherever I might go was second to her.
Why make her feminine? The very gentleness
Of curving packland, warm forested hills
And sparkling winding rivers make her thus.
Born between Severn's bank and Forest green
Mysterious Dean and red banked swirling Severn,
Through blissful childhood, played in dingley dells
Gloucestershire moulded what I was to be.
Grey-stoned churches, and cow-dotted pastures
Gilded my youth. The pastoral scene for me.
It seemed to me that in the years that followed,
Whenever I left the warmth of this my county,
Time upon time trials and disasters followed.
No wonder then when I was free to choose
It was to Gloucestershire that I returned.
Not to the Dean or Severn, though beloved,
But to the Cotswolds and their most enchanting places,
Having the best of worlds, the verge of country,
Leckhampton Hill from out of my bedroom window,
Mysterious, alien invaded territory,
A changing beauty seen through all the seasons,
Yet part of Cheltenham with its Georgian beauty,
And cultural blessings almost without count.
I do love Gloucestershire, and here again
I find enchantment and the peace of childhood.

Barbara Steele

The Joy and Splendour

Wandering down this country lane,
Marvelling at all there is to view,
The flowers in the hedgerow, the calling of the birds,
The fluttering of the many moths and butterflies,
A landscape of varied green, what a truly wonderful scene.

The serenity of this beautiful place,
Woven like a complex tapestry, each blade of grass whispering to
me,
This is Utopia, come listen, look, come see.

Utopia,
The brief occasions, moments, we are at peace with one and all,
Where no anxieties can invade one's thoughts.

Shirley Boyson

75

The Quarry

No earthly spot more fair, rare gem, in setting rare.
This famous ground by Severn's shining ribbon bound.
All steeped in antique mystery, close-knit in Shrewsbury's history.

Source of her ancient walls, her castle, churches, halls.
Place where the active sound of mason's hammers did resound
And later, performed in crude amphitheatre,
The joust and banter of those days or solemn drama (sacred
                                                    Whitsun plays),
And then, so it appears; wasteland for weary years.
Until sublimest art and human ingenuity took part
To clothe in re-creation this erstwhile desolation.
Now place to pause in purest pleasure or lounge in languid leisure;
Absorbing wond'rous views, strolling through avenues
To hear St Chad's sweet chimes steal soft 'neath shading limes;
Where Hercules, beneath the trees, great club at hand, on guard
                                                    doth stand
With solemn mien, while on the green, all glad and gay the
                                                    children play.
In silent tribute stand before memorial grand or listen to a band.
Admire the regulated order of blooms in mixed herbaceous border
Or gaze in awed amaze at rhododendrons' blaze.
Or yet, when scene is set in grand array for Flower Show day,
Among the festive crowds enmingle and view that wonderland
                                                    The Dingle.
Each patterned flower-bed like some bright oriental rug outspread,
And all between cool velvet turf of choicest emerald green;
The fountains playing fling forth a billion diamonds spraying
Such rockeries and spreading trees, such wealth of flowers
                                                    and leafy bowers
Here pool or pond; there fern and frond enfilled the
                                                    archway of archaic guild.

And all the while Sabrina's smile and gaze serene embrace the
                                                        scene.
Most glorious sight, when late at night each fairy light and
                                                    firework bright
With rainbow glow, complete the Show.
Rare gem in setting rare, could Eden be more fair?

Emily Griffiths

An Everyday Tale of Countryfolk Circa 1993

In Bosnia they're killing one another,
Mother, Father, Sister, Brother,
Women who used to shop together,
Children who used to dream . . .
Forever rent apart, from the heart.
For what reason can this be?
No improvement, that is clear to see.
Destruction surrounds their family lives,
Splitting husbands from their wives,
Because this is not a war of need,
It is just a war of greed,
Wanting more than they have got,
Not satisfied with their *lot.*
So, sacrifice the children and their relatives,
This is a battle in which neither side gives,
Life is disposable, a *state of mind,*
Kill them, if they're not our kind.
And what will they gain from this genocide?
A stand, one side, of a great divide,
Condemned by the pacifists of this world,
A manic cruelty they've unfurled.
And they will stand alone one day,
Thinking of things, in a different way.
Perhaps if compassion, they had shown,
Some self-respect, they would own,
But they will go to their graves, knowing,
Some innocent life they are owing . . . Guilty!

Vanessa Morton

Summer Drift

Summer drift, lazy on the air . . .
all perfume, wafting seeded,
light on undersided flash of wings.
Dappled skin, warmly musky against my own,
ripples on water,
mind rustling in unison with the soft-breezed leaves.
It is dreamtime. Unreal. I float on summer sleep,
cushioned by meadows of infant memory.
Summer sleep. Drowsy bee-hummed airless drifting.
Eternal. Timeless. Your skin against my own,
desire trickling into my summer consciousness.
You are here.
Childhood summers, long-gone patterns
of warm grass-sprawled, faintly yearning hours.
Days of endless golden aura fade
and I am here, with you, skin against skin,
hair mingling silken in the grass,
against the earth where insects
survive telescoped replicas of our own short span.
It matters not. I am one with the grass,
with the minute bustling life, with the mounting hot longing,
with the world.
Love me
on this endless hot summer day,
so like and yet so removed from all the others
I have shared with the soft sunlit air.
Love me . . . and this day will shine forever
as the summer I have lost . . .

Sonya Dann

This Town

Memories of this town are very clear
When women drank stout and men mild beer,
Fourpence a pint or was it five
Whichever, it helped keep them all alive.
Shopping was done from open street
Oft soaked to skin from head to feet,
No covered heated walks or squares
Escalators, lifts or mobile chairs.
Shopping trolleys were unheard of then
Nor taxi cabs for Bill or Ben,
Courting was Hemmings entry or Enfield shed
No way for them of sharing a bed.
They had some laughs also frowns
So when you speak of other towns,
Spare a thought for those who planned
The precinct, the palms, the weekly band.
Think how dull life may have been
Without this ever changing scene.

A Avery

Wyeside Drama

It was such a pleasant winter scene
As cormorants plied the waters clear,
And the old alder stood so calm, serene.
But now the dreaded fog is here

And the old dead alder shows alarm
As in that ghostly fog it looms.
Its branches look like panic stricken arms
Flung wide to the encircling gloom.

Strange birds the murky waters search
And for their hapless prey they dive.
Then one by one they fly up to perch
To the old alder's lofty hive.

They spread their wings, in ominous design,
Their long necks they turn and twist.
It's as though some stark and morbid sign
Is etched on that dark shroud of mist.

The curtain falls, our birds disappear,
But from the gloom strange voices rise.
Are they of the ghosts of yesteryear
Or just the cormorants' restless cries?

John Keyse

Poem of Gloucester

Drifting on air,
This horseless carriage
Making a timeless
Never ending voyage
Through the muddy
Waters of time
History's story repeated,
The bells peeling lowly,
Calling the faithful nigh,
Westgate Street held its breath,
The frost a carpet
Where unknown feet once walked
Lined the streets.
Their shadows pulling invisible shawls
Across invisible shoulders,
Side by side with flesh and blood people
In their pullovers and fur lined boots.
The shops lined this city's streets
Like brick soldiers on parade,
Their shutters, all seeing eyes to
Times momentum,
Closed.
Superfluous to the gulls calling lowly
The faithful nigh.
Southgate Street took its breath and choked
On its fumes lingering with its
Buildings that stood proudly.
They've fallen, like toppled kings
Their reign now over,
Leaving their shadows kissing
Shadowy children
Off to work along with their flesh
And blood counterparts.

Susan Broadbent

Kings of the Forest

I stood before this mass of living cells
Gazing at shapes each arm would take;
Something deep, way deep inside compels
Me to breathe the chlorophyll of life which wake
The pulses of the brain, here within the cranium.

Oh man! Whom God so kindly did these beauties made,
Can you not hear them in their anguish cry?
Leave us rested clutching the sods where we are laid
To be a take-off point from where birds do fly.

And then again, content to be a focal point for Man and Maid
Who stand and view the blossoms in our hair come spring,
Or, on a summer's day, may find some shade
Beneath the boughs, and watch the birds on wing;

Then with the autumn's changing hue,
Our leaves portray the joy we gave
All spring and summer thro'.
Come winter time, the snow does pave
Our limbs which when the sun does touch,
Sparkles and glistens as in fairy tales
To give glee to children and such
Until shaken clean by gales.

So leave us be, and let us please,
If only in your solitude to gaze;
Or a saddened soul we can appease
And a lowly spirit we will raise.

Norah Stoker

Our Ancestral Home

O English rose, your regal pose
Those eternal roots of our ancestral home
An old rustic arch where brambles climb
Sky larks still sing their love song in rhyme.
O England, how your beauty prevails
Can it ever fail yet only compel.
While I secretly walk down cobble stone lanes
Soft rolling hills make picturesque frames,
This fragrant breath is nothing less
Than you, O England.
A proud smile on your face as I travel to trace
Never lose that dignity or historical taste,
Great memories unfold in those castles of old
Exploring through corridors, the chronicles behold
You, O England.
As a lady in waiting greets her King to kneel
The court jester entertains us with bells on his heels.
Fair maidens run tittering across the grounds, all a gaze
They hide themselves quickly in that huge green dense maze,
Looking back for a moment my imaginative heart played
Whilst the essence of the atmosphere fell upon me as rain
O English rose, such sweet perfume
Your delicate petals so proud in bloom.
You reign forever outside my room
Of our ancestral home.

Susan Slavinec

Spring

See, beneath the melting snow,
The grass still green,
And rivers flow
Where once was seen
A glassy stream,
The fresh sprung snowdrop
Bows its head,
To manifest
A winter shed
Of all its chills,
And coughs and cries,
Whilst daffodils
Will soon arise,
Like golden stars
In gay profusion,
After the winter's
White confusion,
And fields of lambs
Will, with their bleating
Give this new year
A final greeting.

R Russell

A Country Life

The countryside is the life for me
Open air and fancy free,
Cotswold hills a sea of corn
With waves that break on limestone walls.
No high rise blocks or fast food bars
Not choked by fumes from passing cars,
Sun rays warm the lichen stone
Of tall church spires that stand alone.
He sits on high the weather cock
I envy that view from his seat on top,
Alas to see the sun go down
To shroud such beauty all around.
Small bats awake as darkness falls
And dodge the stars with twittering calls.
So if in the cities I have to stay
There is one thing that I must say,
The Cotswold hills shall you see
Be a place my heart will yearn to be.

Roger Stokes

Central England

Central England shire counties
Hark back to a *halcyon age*
When things were left as they were;
No homes for homeless or handicapped
In their sheltered closes and verdant fields.

Where did the homeless and handicapped live then I wonder?
In ditches where they died perhaps,
Or off to the city,
Out of sight and out of mind
Of Central England shire counties.

G Holt

Untitled

A city so grey, but so red,
deepest emotions being shed.
The truth, the sublime,
join this time.
Lost and endangered motions,
festival commotions.
Reality losing its way,
the future's coming
let it pass.

Steve Manchester

At Home on the Hill

Coughing, the bark of sheep,
in the early morning of still darkness
damp warmth, wet from a lull
of winter's nigh.
Soft spring the bank turf rising
toward the track mud tractor churned.
Lift and swing the heavy iron gate
whose hefty post support has loosened
jarred from its fulcrum by man tall tyres.
Opening the lock full of rain drops stored
as the early day wet slants down;
securing the doors ajar against the wind.
Feeling my way to unlock the driver's door
to rotate the stalk creating a vision of day
through the end of the last day's night.
Start up, reverse and change rubber
to leather, closing the doors and turn
into the fog tinged dark and work.
Across country, three counties, ninety miles
driving to the rising sun and morning
of a new day whose labours secure the home.
The balanced still of rural calm equates
each mile of close attention, day of work
to so relax, adjust, live quietly together.

Edward L Gray

To Sapperton

Which way? This way, the sign says Daneway,
Along the towpath beneath the railway
The Frome flows freely, tinkling. Really!
Murmuring, gurgling, gushing, rushing
Through the race where waterwheels turned in its pushing
Blocks of stone now green with moss,
While everything else is white with frost
Dear God it's cold - But the brave and bold are out in force
Following the course of the overgrown and derelict canal.

In a field, a tiny hut, its doors and windows firmly shut
The beechnuts crunching underfoot,
or frosted glass as thick as snow
Which sounds as though your careful feet
Are trampling through a giant's box of shredded wheat.

The silence deafens when standing still
The slightest sound is all it takes
and from the hill the pigeons flap in panicked flight across the lake
Where Bee the Otter swims on bright and sunny days
Faerie grottoes, Elfish scenes, through a bower laced with reeds
Overhanging evergreens and fluffy puffs of clematis seeds
Finches, Wrens and Robins feed.

The woodland high looks down on man upon the path
and whispers welcome from the ridge
As passing by, we raise our sights
and gaze in awe at such majestic pride
Over bridges, through a gate,
Keeping up the steady rate of one step forward, stop and see,
No leaves to flutter if indeed there were a breeze.

But myriad sparkles in the sun - Mother Nature's bit of fun
A tree of diamonds: only to be touched by wonder's eyes
Then miniature rainbows one by one and bye and bye
With an onomatopoeic *plink*, dissolve to liquid
Makes you think of magic.

And so at last to brief respite, a half of ale both clear and light
Then half a mile to journey's end:
The tunnel where the leggers used to bend to aching toil
An ancient cottage crumbling to the soil
We shout, 'Halloo,' and wait, but no reply
So with a sigh we turn and wish the wish goodbye
Retracing steps in going home.

John W Lang

The Turn of the Tide

The long, flat beach stretches out to the calm turquoise sea,
Covered in a desert of golden sand.
A wave of brightly coloured sunshades and windbreakers,
Stretch as far as the eye can see.
Rock-pools, hand scattered across the beach,
Shelter a motley collection of sea creatures,
Trapped by the rapid departure of the tide.
Pebbles and shells in an array of colours,
The majority of which form a steady line,
A little wavy in places,
Where the turning tide deserted them.
A motion reversed.
The calm sea comes splish-splashing onto the shore,
in small, steady waves, rebounding off the sand,
As the orange sun gradually sinks lower and lower
Deeper and deeper,
Further and further into the dark icy waters.
The crowds decrease, then all depart,
All except one stray dog, running wild and free,
splashing in rock-pools.
As the tide continues to turn.

Neil Cleland (12)

Husbands Bosworth

Trustee trees robe entrance
From the Leicester side,
Expectancy rises
As I climb the hill
Past gracious Fernie Lodge,
Whiskered time lolls on walls,
Chimes away generations
In cool dreaming rooms.

Entering from Market Harborough side
Much is promised here,
The ornate toll-house
Now stands back retired.
Round the spacious bend
The honeyed church startles,
Then in her splendour
Uplifts, leads me in.

Norman Harrington

Late Spring in Polly Botts Lane

Sunshine on a celandine
Primroses, wood anemones,
Daylight stars
Reflect blue sky.

Tree pipit
Like a paper dart,
Sends off a rival
Courting his mate.

Inside the wood
Bluebells,
Startle us
With their presence.

The wind shakes them
Nobody picks them
They belong here,
To surprise us.

Anne Kind

The Snowdrop

The little snowdrop,
Bows its head.
Over the old leaves,
Brown and dead.
Soon it will be
Joining them there,
Leaving this world,
Full of worry and care.

I often wonder,
What my fate will be,
Of how I shall die,
And be set free.
No one will tell us,
What's coming our way.
Or that each morning,
Might be our last day.

So like the flowers,
And all things around,
My bones will perish,
And mingle in the ground,
But my soul,
And the good things I've done,
Will live on forever,
My life's work then done.

Peggy Mason

Leafy Warwickshire

When Mother Nature looked around
a long, long time ago
she was seeking out the fairest place
her bounty to bestow.
In a flash of inspiration
she made for England's shore
and there, right in the centre,
found what she was looking for.

So she planted out her garden
with oak and ask and pine,
providing shelter from the storm
and shade when it was fine.
Then she remembered fruit trees
and apple, plum and pear
she added to the landscape
with green fields everywhere.

As she saw what she'd created
with the help of rain and sun
she named it leafy Warwickshire,
then when the job was done
she said, 'This is my masterpiece
it will never be surpassed,'
and she signed it *Mother Nature*
her task complete at last.

Irene Hopper

Gloucester Canal

(Dedicated to Ricky)

Smells have been missed,
As in a car I have always travelled;
But here on a boat, on a river,
I see the world through the eyes -
Of an audience watching a film.

It is as if I can walk on water -
as though I have found my faith,
In this boat, on this canal,
This place that was once -
as busy as the town's roads are now.

Here is peace, here has nature along the sides,
Here is sanctuary on which I can hide -
from those hectic roads, those crowded streets,
Here I can smell the air.
The boat, the river and me - nothing more than we three.

Janice Vaughan

Moonlight Sonata

(Coventry 1940 - 1990 November 14th remembered)

Autumn leaves
drifting from silent pinnacles of grief:
each leaf, a life
each spreading vein, the lifeblood
of an eager soul
seared in the flame of war . . .
curling in sadness
on Cathedral stone.

Yet out of darkness
came forth Paradise
and sunlight, imbued
with windowed reds and blues
transcends the gloom -
each modest leaf
made glorious
in that shining hour.

In chapelled calm
a lone musician fingers *Moonlight*
while glassy saints,
their trumpets raised,
gaze down in triumph
and are glad.

Josie Davies

Winter

Snow twirling round and round
Softly falling to the ground,
On the lamp posts by your door
Come on snowflakes I want more.

Children playing bright and gay
What a wonderful, super day,
Suddenly it's all gone dark
It is black all over the park.

Night-time's come it's time for bed
'Come on children,' mother said,
Children slowly climb the stairs
Poor old snowmen, no one cares.

In the morning what a sight
It's not snowing there's no bright light,
Children wetting the floor with tears
No applause and no great cheers.

Lauretta Young

Shrewsbury

We're lucky to live in Shrewsbury,
It's a really interesting place,
Loads of history, a river,
And plenty of open space.

Buildings with timbers of black and white,
A castle above the station,
The Abbey, St Chads, the Quarry,
It's such a beautiful location.

The Dingle in the Quarry,
Full of shrubs and flowers,
They're sculling on the river,
That circles this town of ours.

A haven for the tourists,
Many from overseas,
Pubs and restaurants round the Square,
The cafes for cream teas.

A pretty town to visit,
Ideal for a holiday,
So have a look at Shrewsbury,
Like us, maybe, you'll stay.

Steve Woodman

Through the Window

I look out of the window,
Not a happy sight.
A blanket of fallen snowflakes.
So crunchy, crisp and white.

The landscape is anaemic,
Few colours to be seen.
The branches are so laden,
They start to bend and lean.

The paths are wet and icy,
People tumble in a heap.
The coldness overwhelms me,
It makes my warm skin creep.

The weather is appalling,
A scene of gloom and woe.
The sky is bleak and wintry,
An omen of more snow.

But that's what's out the window,
I'm warm here in my class,
It's really rather cosy,
On this side of the glass!

Rory Broomfield (14)

Maytime

Winter is many months of the year
But now at last Maytime is here;
And birds sing from a leafy screen
In the tree and hedgerow freshly green;
And the wood-anemone is out in the shade,
With its blushing petals which too soon fade;
Once more the bracken is unfurling there,
And bluebells gently perfume the damp air.

Once more golden buttercups blow in the field,
And among the flowers young children kneel.
Once more wild chervil bedecks with white lace
Each grassy hollow and wayside place;
And the cuckoo calls across the land . . .
How welcome is its curious sound;
And how glad I am to see
Blossom appear upon the hawthorn tree.

V A Twells

Gainsborough Spa

You've heard about Harrogate spa
people go there to replenish their health,
we nearly had one in Gainsborough
in those days there wasn't much wealth.
Now there is cash right above it
the Kings theatre is built there you see,
people play bingo for cash now
where a ghost walks at night probably.
The lord of the manor took his bath first
that was the rule at the time,
no matter how long the queue was
they all had to wait there in line.
It was a very popular place
people came here from near and from far,
to get the medicinal properties
from this amazing spa.
Then a man called Revell was murdered most horrid
his body was dumped in the spring,
nobody came here anymore
popularity dropped off quite rapid.
So the next time that you go to the Kings
just think of the place where you are,
instead of playing bingo
you could be sitting in the spa.

Marjorie Mary Pearson

More Canals Than Venice

A sprawling glass topped
concrete rooted
smoke succumbed
animal;
breathing and relaxing
gearing up at four pm
to congeal into
revving rush hour impatience.

Alyson Faye

Snow Walk

We walked from Rearsby to Frisby along the river Wreake.
The river in its wide meandering, lay still
Dull, and shallowly frozen.
Our feet creak-crunched and slid in snow
Ankle, calf and thigh deep.

The snow, silver-flaked, lay dimpled
Smooth and wide, unmarked except by tracks.
Here rabbits dashed through hedge gap,
Foxes, trotted in wide curves,
There moorhens pattered in hedge bottoms,
Blackbird wingmarks lay like fingers in the quiet snow.

Red-tiled roofs edged with white ribbon
Gathered quietly by their centrepiece churches.
The wet track from Rotherby to Brooksby
Was burnished gold by the setting sun.
The sky turned from blue to grey to pink
At the end of the short day.

Gill Ball

This is My Home

I am home here
 amid the rolling hills;
The beauty of the valleys
 is a treasure trove of thrills;
The scene is ever changing,
 something new to see each day
A happy place to come back to
 when I have been away.
And though I love to travel
 to countries with warmer clime,
When I return
 I look around
And say,
 'These hills are mine.'
For while I've taken pleasure
 in scenes from distant lands,
And spent long sunny lazy days
 on other's golden sands,
These Cotswolds have a beauty
 that give a better prize,
And returning from my travels
 I view them with fresh eyes.

Cynthia Dickens

Leicester C-1860

The roof slopes, the boxed chimneys.
The factory stacks
Fingering smudges into the sky.
St Margaret's odd corner,
The tower of the Scottish Queen.
A line of shadow from the Globe,
All down Silver Street,
To, the space where the Clock Tower
Isn't.
And carts, and gigs, and no people.
Trees in the city, but no men.

Hitler missed you.
Town planners didn't.
Flower baskets, now, in Loseby Lane.

Chris Challis

Rutland

The rape seed sways
violent yellow,
in rough flat fields
where rivers wind.

A low brushed light
sweeps the white sky,
above the shallow
scented spinneys.

Beyond the trees
Stone villages shelter,
where absent bells
chime through meadows.

The clear air lush
with wildflowers.
Where birds circle
to spear the sunlight,

hedged roads curve
and pause for simple hump bridges.

Christopher Stickley

New Life

I am but a dandelion seed in the wind
Light and fluffy - so free . . .
But there's always the rain to wash me away
I am but a dandelion seed in a stream
Wet and broken - so sad . . .
Eventually washed up on to a bank
Where into new life I will grow
I am but a dandelion seed in the ground
Struggling, struggling for freedom
Sunshine, please hurry, gentle breeze too
I am but a dandelion seed in the wind . . .

J Smith

May Morning

I like the still neat little green rows
punctuating the damp soil, the inch high
semi-colons of beans spaced in order
carrots a line of exclamation
marks tight in their form;
though chickweed and vetch misprint
my prim paragraph, I the compsitor mind
my peas like question marks uncurling.
Look! here's a dotted line of lettuce
no higher than Tom Thumb; here's
a flourish, a demanding marrow,
a vivid cucumber, an ampersand;
tomatoes in this dawn illuminated
capitals proudly standing. Hoeing and raking
such nice orthography, such syntactical
eight point splendour, I tend
to admire the mysterious author.

Simon Baynes

Still for Sale

I gazed at you for quite a while
Before I entered in.
I thought this isn't just a house
It lives to fight and win.
The key released the creaking door.
To reveal what I would see.
And then I felt the icy blast
That wrapped itself round me.
Shivering I slowly walked
Towards an empty room.
The closed door slowly opened
I stepped into the gloom.
The nightmare that awaited me
That second did begin
The door slammed hard behind me
The very walls did reek
Of all that's foul, no mess to see.
Just death, decay confronting me.
Dear God I screamed save me from this
The door stuck fast. The icy blast
My interest was all done
And then the push with screaming force.
Through open door I fell
Out in the street I stood and wept
That old grim house had won.

Anne Matthews

A Sonnet

Now when we sleep we dream of forgetting.
Where once the sunlight cast its welcome gaze,
A world in darkness shorn of seasons setting
Forever winter with its bitter haze.
We plant a seed and pray for its dear life
To flourish in the unavailing years,
We struggle on and on in spite of strife,
And water it with our own blood stained tears.

Then all at once our hope begins to flower
And sprout its new green shoots so far and wide,
The mighty deluge softens to a shower,
And peace and love now blossom side by side.
And in the morn the waking eye may see
The spring buds bursting forth eternally.

Andrew Paton

A Place of Quiet Understanding

Walk with me a while
and we'll talk a worried mile
to a place of quiet understanding.

We'll not talk of Trees
or of the Birds and Bees,
But instead of the way things really are.

About how simple pain is
and how cynicism burns humanity,
until there's nothing to do but shatter illusions.

Until the only comfort left is testing
the endurance of your own tired senses,
or scraping your nerves 'til they jangle.

I know you can never return to that
Wondrous place of shattering discovery
of electrically charged delusion where everything is virgin.

Still nothing shocks any more
we've seen the full repertoire
of humanity's dirty death ridden land.

There is no Heaven, no blissful existence
except when I've taken your hand,
and we've finished our walking, our talking
and we both understand, all we have is each other.

Mark Dale

The Castle

Through a labyrinth of moss covered passages
And dappled beauty from the shadowed trees
I came upon a castle.
Its pride was etched in every stone.
Columned and arched
Ruling over the countryside
In regal splendour,
Acknowledging the change
Itself unchanging.
Speaking with silent words
Of other times,
When rumbling carriages approached
Jostling through the night air
And glowing chandeliers shone out their welcome.
Smooth velvet and rich brocade
Rustling silks and satins
Jewel coloured against the sombre stone.
Pampered privilege.
Its blinded eyes could see beyond
To overcrowded rows of shared yards,
And candle shadowed rooms with smoking fires
Where children lived in patchwork poverty
And laughed and played,
Who knew no other life.
And mothers and fathers
Took comfort from them
And love and care
Each for the other,
Shone through all that was unfair
And strengthened their fierce pride.
I strolled reluctantly
Along the dusty drive,
To leave behind the past
To reconstruct the present.

T L Robinson

God Gave Me Eyes to See

Lawn daisies facing sunwards,
welcoming the daylight hours
with a myriad of tiny petals . . .
A hundred shades of green,
as trees toss and bounce in the wind,
shaking their leaves in merriment;
or turned to lace as winter's frost
paints each leaf with masterful artistry . . .
The shining eyes of children
reflected in Christmas baubles,
which promise the most magical of times
It little ones who wait,
anticipating promised treats . . .
Rough seas crashing against sea walls,
or trying to break the rocky shores
which stand resolved and firm against the storm . . .
A mother bird with chicks in nest,
caring, sharing the morsels of nourishment
she has sought and found;
raising her brood to maturity
in just a few short weeks . . .
Rich colours of leaves in autumn,
which fall to be trampled underfoot,
creating a joyful, crackling sound . . .
Blackbirds calling to each other in song,
as day turns to dusk and then to night . . .
Painted skies, sunsets, rainbows . . .
God gave me eyes to see
and I cherish such sights as these.

Margaret Worsley

Lost Landscapes

The room is clean, white, mercifully bare,
free from the fripperies and foibles of other ladies' rooms.
No photographs crowd the tables,
no pictures mar the walls.
Even the shadows retreat from the soft sunlight.
And at her window she sits, she always sits,
watching the world go by,
silent and smiling in the warm afternoon.

Green gardens curl out from her window,
dotted and starred with late summer flowers,
and a woody lane carries life away.
She sees the old people walk past, sometimes,
tired and frail. Their weary eyes
look into hers, sometimes.
Young people come and go, wearing serious faces
even behind their smiles,
fearing their expectant youth an intrusion.
And still she sits smiling in the warm afternoon.

Her family come to visit sometimes,
but she doesn't need them now.
In the blankness of her mind she is content,
her eyes reflecting scenes that march by her window,
not remembering the past,
not hoping for a future.
It is only others who need to search
for lost landscapes in her mind.

Kristina Moore

The Forgotten Barricade

I am wandering in that place,
Where the curtain of atrocities cover,
Where there are cries of the many innocent,
Where there is a thirst for more blood and more pointless lives.

I am wandering in that place,
Where the good never rules,
Where the bad always rises to the surface,
Where the innocent suffer,
Where the homeless orphans witness merciless war.

I am wandering in that place,
Where you see but not believe,
Where you ask yourself why,
Where suffering and anguish live every minute of every day,
Where the powerful sit back and indulge in maliciousness.

I am wandering in that place,
and I want to know why,
Why nobody lifts a finger to stop this tragedy,
Why nobody stands by innocent victims,
Why nobody stops this bloody war.

Shaheen Akhtar

Here in Suffolk

They may say *were country folk* and life for us is dull!
But do they know what our counties like, or why we love it so?

Well if your time is empty, and to relax you must, put your
hopes and fears behind and travel here to us.
There is so much to offer, the choices vast and wide, to stay
in thatch, or country house, a windmill if inclined.

We also have the Orwell, a river strong and true, it rushes
along beneath its bridge, where ships and boats pass through.
The town of Ipswich holds such treasures of times that
passed us by, the ancient house, the Great white horse, where
Pickwick once did lie.

Haunted places here to search, trees of plenty beech to
birch, open spaces, hills to climb, sandy beaches, lanes entwined.
Worth a visit I'm sure you'll see, why this county means
so much to me.

Julie Ketley

East Lindsey Marshes

These marsh flats lie to the Eastern side
Where the sea, like a mother, caresses its shore.
And bracing winds blow back inland, polluted fumes,
Industry's dusts and spoils,
Keeping this infant land
Fresh, sweet, free and pure.

Nature's world lives here unfettered by human touch.
Natterjack toads, rare and beautiful orchids,
Rabbits scurrying into their burrows,
Foxes chasing sunset shadows.

All sorts of creatures live in this sodden dish.
Owls flutter above their victims
While herons stop and pause to fish.
Terns rise, then dive, down into gorse.
Pheasants play out in the open
And insects sing aloud in verse.
Migrating ducks or geese who come for temporary stays
Mingle with swans who sail on its waterways.

I often walk on its thick grassy blanket,
Clearing my head of anxieties,
Allowing its peace and tranquillity
To wash me over clean.
It soothes my soul, so,
I'm repaired fit to face again
The life of man with his insanity.

Stephen Beaumont

Lincolnshire

On verge in woods the snowdrops lie,
A vision to delight the eye,
As daffodils stand tall and bold
A cloth of gold soon clothes the wold.
While cherry trees in pink and white
Create a scene of pure delight,
In Lincolnshire spring's glorious bounty
Beautifies this ancient county.
The summer scene brings fields of green
And poppies bright with scarlet gleam,
The oilseed rape of golden hue
Offset with linseed lakes of blue.

Betty Crowcombe

Four Seasons of Essex

The sweet smelling air tells us when spring is here
The green fields of Essex seem soft and sincere.
Its pastures are moist with the soft morning dew
  and the lambs frisk about as if somehow they knew.
I love this dear county, I know her so well
  it would take me too long for strange stories to tell.

Gardens look colourful, cheery and bright -
  the fragrance of blooms stays through the night.
Blue skies in daytime, red skies at night
  these are the things that make summer just right.
Essex is beautiful, Essex is true
Where is there another county like you?

Leaves start to fall and a carpet is made of the finest
  of leaves in a brown rusty shade.
Hedgerows are tinted like dark auburn hair
  and colours of autumn made softly aware.
Landscapes of Essex, a wonderful sight -
  at this time of year it's an artist's delight.

The scenery changes from brown to pure white
  and pastures are covered with snow overnight.
The duck-ponds are frozen and icicles form on the branches
  of trees, just before dawn.
In the depth of deep winter the softness remains
  'til the green leaves return in the quiet Essex lanes.

Doreen P Francis-Ewen

Our Suffolk Heritage

No golden treasure found here of Tutankamun,
But a golden treasure found of a different kind,
In these grassy mounds and flowing sand-dunes,
Along this unique shingle and sandy coast will find,
Wild flowers, butterflies and rare birds in flight,
And the swish, swish of reeds and grasses in the breeze,
Gentle sloping cliffs and bracken kiss the sea and bite,
The ever changing erosion of the coast like a big cheese,
Crumbling and slithering into the jaws of the North-Sea,
And through and through the peace, soothing like balm,
Away from the crowds and the curse of the Sadducees,
Where we sup mother nature and breath in her charms.

David Dawrant

Wandering

Colours of sunrise fading in the afternoon,
As the pastel painted sky hides behind towering trees,
And daytime lays down its weary head,
All that moves now is the whispering breeze.

As night-time shrouds this cherished place,
The bustling villages take their rest,
The countryside shadows spring to life,
As hunter and prey begin their quest.

Villages united by wandering paths,
With old houses beamed and bent,
Delicate cottages built so long ago,
Now bow like an elderly gent.

People here remember the times gone by,
The views are fuel for their dreams,
Breathing life into stories,
Of open spaces and lonely streams.

Weathered faces have immortalised,
The land for which they strived,
To recall its unique beauty,
And keep the past alive.

Wandering through this land so vast,
Timeless are the scenes,
Man would never encounter boredom,
Only the beauty of what he sees.

Beverley Mahon

Waterfowl

Evenings their swift and raucous grace
Shrinks to fit the receptive arc of dusk.
Afloat they jack-knife into dormant space,
Moulding their clay against some tree-root tusk.
Cheeping young scoot to pennate side
While mother opens up a rear-view eye,
Chill basilisk surveying all her pride,
Drugged but wakeful in her watery sty.
Clouds engage the peeling rim of night,
Shallower than the stars in filmy strength.
At dawn lightning lifts the lid of sky,
Discovering stones along the sedge's length.

A J Wells

Norwich - Welcome to a Fine City

Cobblestone roads.
Houses built so close as to be almost kissing overhead.
Dark doorways beckoning, treasure laden shops,
almost forgotten under modern day dust.

Puppies, black and playful amongst the green finery,
Overhanging branches brushing the tops of commuter's heads.
Onlookers smile in the hazy sunlight - intent on exploration,
Not noticing the traffic and the postcards, drinking in the beauty.
Quaintness unchanged through time's progress.
Old and new lying so close together, not clashing, but living in
harmony.
Dukes and tramps have all walked this city's streets - a fine one,
Turning another corner only to find something totally unexpected
Whether it be a dustcart wending its way around the tiny streets
Or an antique clock chiming its daily time over a supermarket door.
It's all here - only to find it, you need time and patience.

Surrounded by marshland infested with windmills and ducks,
The tranquillity disturbed only by the harsh beating, of the
heron's lonely vigil,
Watching over the broadlands.
Which gives way to the outlying suburbs,
Leading to the tall majestic building at the top of the hill,
Keeping guard over Norwich, as it has done for centuries,
Neighbour to the regal cathedral,
Full of gaping, open-mouthed grockles wondering at the
history of this monument.
Still standing, still watching,
Over Elm Hill, the Mustard Shop, Brideswell Alley,
The market place in front of the town hall steps,
Near the fountain that falls whilst children throw their pennies in
Half expecting the goldfish to swallow them.
All this and more, in Norwich - a fine city,
Welcome to Norwich.

Carol M Willis

After a Storm at West Runton

Like a vulture
The ravenous sea
Has picked the bones,
Of this once house
Clean and bare.

Just a table leg
Lies alone on the sand
And above the twisted.
Jumbled mass of once fence
Sandcastled to the beach.

In a high fissure, newly-made,
Against a blue spring sky
Two fulmars, snow white
Of breast, long of wing,
Have made their nest.

I hear them now
Cackling their new-found joy.
Joyous their mating song,
As the savage sea, far below,
Cradles their cries.

Richard Stewart

The Cliffs at Walton

A vista of blue, shimmering sea
Kites fly, larks tremble on high.
The cliffs red-gold
sandwiched with blue clay
are crowned with a summer hat
of grass and flowers.
But surely the path is narrower
than yesterday?
The relentless, rolling surge of the sea
devours beneath, unseen.
Slowly the earth slides, a gentle avalanche.
Like a child's half-eaten biscuit
bite-sized chunks fall crumbling,
jam-topped with pink willow-herb.
Above, the short, dry grass
moves in the breeze, not sensing danger.
The lark sings on, a chorister at this marriage
of land and sea.

Nancy Johnson

Essex

Essex?
Yes, it's flat isn't it?
Busy and noisy - I've been to Ilford and Romford.

Yes, but - have you ever climbed the hill into Maldon
or seen the Essex marshes?
Maybe you've never stood on the Strood at Mersea
watching the tide come in.

Essex accent -
You come from London don't you?
No my dear,
I say ennert - not innit
and rabber' - not rabbi'
A longer, lazier drawl.

More contrasts?
Take Colchester in particular.
It's Roman armies giving way to Her Majesty's
It's Dutch Quarter almost lost among the people
and the shopping precincts.
Its Oyster Feast attended by commuters and countrymen alike.
A perfect combination of old and new.

Essex?
I love it.

Margaret Williams

Suffolk My Home

I've roamed a good many places both abroad and in this land
But I've yet to see a county with the countryside so grand
A day out can take you on a visit to Southwold, Flatford, or Clare
The whole place is rich is history, I can imagine the battles there.

Cromwell commanded his soldiers, to ruin the churches so old
They tried in vain to burn them down, but never succeeded, I'm told.
The racegoers who visit Newmarket, put their shirt on and
                                        hope for the best
If their horse comes home first they are cheering, if not their
                                        money's gone west.

Fathers and sons at the weekend, from Nayland and Wiston it
                                        seems,
Go off to Ipswich all lively, to cheer for their football teams.
Sunday afternoons in springtime, with husband and dog in tow,
You'll find me walking up Gravel Hill, to Stoke where the bluebells
                                        grow.

The field at the end of my garden brings the seasons each in their
                                        turn,
To provide us with endless enjoyment, its beauty too precious to
                                        spurn.
Whether it be snow in winter, or the harvest with pheasants so rare
I make time to watch the wildlife, their antics too quaint to compare.

Constable painted his landscapes, of the Stour, millstream or farm,
And a portrait of Christ in Nayland Church, on the altar
                                        where all is so calm.
Wherever I go on my travels, be it Dublin, Zurich or Rome
I know when I reach the airport, I'll soon be back in lovely
                                        Suffolk my home.

Olive Willingale

The Riches of the Norfolk Broads

It is the old-fashioned canoe I fancy;
The lovely streamlined, smooth way to proceed
As, with one paddle, the dip turned deftly,
The slim prow is bought in line to lead
Into the quieter reaches: just as easily
Halted, to rest in cool beds of reed,
Where, if one keeps still, absolutely,
One can watch a crafty heron feed,
Or blue jewelled blaze, breast fiery
Kingfisher, plunging to satisfy its greed
For minnows, to poise majestically,
Clear of eddying water, reflected: deed
Accomplished with precisive accuracy.
Tiny silver shoals, without apparent heed,
Are clearly visible above the sinuously
Undulating gold or sombre waterweed.
Such tranquil moments come but rarely.
The Affluent Society, without apparent heed,
Conveyed by motor-boats, sleek and noisy,
Split the surface *going places* at great speed,
Wakes slapping all awash appallingly.
Not for these the life of sleepy timeless mead,
The play of light, the beauty of a willow tree.
Radios blare; they have everything they need
To drown boredom and deadening monotony.
The materialists are not a welcome breed.
Last refuge where scarce, resplendent breed,
The Swallowtail, lay ova on the rare Milk Parsley,
And booming Bittern stealthily concealed in reed
Now so very seldom heard in dwindling sanctuary.

N Creina Glegg

I Love Suffolk

I love Suffolk, what more can I say?
A wonderful place, to work and to play,
The countryside is not very far
Only a short journey in my car.
Where bird's will sing and rabbits hop
Where the whole wide world just seems to stop,
Where the rivers ripple on their way
And along the banks butterflies play,
It's so quiet and as peaceful as can be
And all that can be heard is the humming of a bee.
Suffolk's the prettiest county of all
Where trees just seem to grow so tall,
And pretty little cottages, dot the green
Can't you just imagine the beautiful scene?
A wonderful landscape in your mind's eye
Yes I love Suffolk and now you know why!

Dawn Morgan

131

Burghley in September

Misty morning in September
Horses champ the dew rich grass
Snorting with their nostrils flaring,
The lake is calm and clear as glass.
Stately Burghley stands majestic
Its numerous windows are like eyes,
Gazing down on lush green parkland
And great gnarled oaks reach the skies
Air now fills with bustling chatter
Bridles gleam and saddles shine,
Horses canter with tails aswishing
Tossing heads and mane so fine.
People many miles have travelled
This annual meeting is renowned,
Foreign tongue and local dialect
All at Burghley can be found.
Horse Trials come and soon are over
Familiar faces come and go,
Friendships made and hands are shaken
'Til next year and another show.

Carolyn Fraser

View From My Window

Corn, bleached almost white,
Long August shadows,
Willows and horse chestnuts,
Stand in the distance,
Behind telegraph poles,
And rows of blackened beans.
Beyond, more corn,
Lightens the landscape,
Pylons petrified,
Like six armed giants,
Clouds above,
Stacked in white kingdoms,
On summer evenings.
The pepperpot, over Linton,
Red and grey,
On a rounded hilltop,
A village symbol,
The highest landmark.

Sarah Linklater

Colchester

There's a sign beside the road,
On the outskirts of the town
It says in letters big and bold
Britain's Oldest Recorded Town
The Romans came so long ago,
The Ancient Britons made to tow
The line and do just as they said,
Or for sure they'd lose their heads!
Then Boudicca took up the fight
She fought and fought with all her might.
They razed the temple to the ground,
And then they marched 'til Romans found
A battle fought but it was lost
You couldn't see the Brits for dust!

C A Pinfold

Call of the Wild

'Tis not the county of my birth
This lavish slice of Essex earth,
But here I am and here I'll stay
Absorbing beauty day by day.
Golden cornfields meadows green
No wonder artists scan the scene,
Rich stocked rivers flow toward sea
Wildlife abundant roam over lea.
Sails in the sunset flit o'er the meres
Watermills treading, pulsating weirs,
Shimmering sand shellfish galore
Elegant waders searching the shore.
Herbs for all cooking, elder for wine,
Yes by golly Essex's sublime!

Iris Jean Smith

Autumn Fields

The corn is cracking in the hot sun,
And mice are panicking, it is time to run,
The Harvester arrives and begins its work,
Noisy business cutting each stalk,
Then neatly stacked and left to dry,
Food for winter, an abundant supply.

Jean Davies

136

Colchester

I was born and bred in Colchester
It's Britain's oldest recorded town,
A town so full of history
I decided to track it down.

The town dates back to the iron age
The Romans came in Fifty Four BC,
There are roman walls and dungeons
Still standing today I see.

Bodicea she came to Colchester
The year was Fifty One AD,
Killing everyone in sight
Traces of the battle remain to see.

The Romans left in the Fifth century
A Saxon town Colchester was made,
And throughout its many years
It remained a town of trade.

The Normans came in Ten Sixty Six
They built a castle oh so fine,
It still stand now in Castle Park
Hardly changing with the pass of time.

Then came the Roundheads and the Cavaliers
Who laid siege in Sixteen Forty Eight,
You can still see the bullet holes
At the Siege House near East Gates.

Colchester's still changing now
Its history for all to see,
Come and have a look yourself
It might surprise you as it did me.

John F Connor

Eastern Men

What can I write about East Anglia?
Where my love affair began.
Where Britons, Romans, Angles, Saxons
Made the Eastern man.

Slow, thinking men, independent and sure
Who look you straight in the eye,
They're the salt of the earth these Anglian men
With courage you cannot buy!

Maybe at dawn when the sun's ne're awake
You're strolling along the fields,
You'll meet him - a gun tucked under his arm with
A faithful old dog at his heels.

He'll be tall or short, sandy hair and blue eyes
He will speak with a slow old twang,
You'll know from the brogue, the gun and the dog
That he is an Eastern man.

Off times along the seashore way,
In the cobbled lokes and lanes,
You'll meet him again - you'll know for sure
He's descended direct from the Danes!

Do they still survive these Eastern Men?
These modest men we know?
Surviving the ravaging Eastern sea?
The Anglian winds that blow?

Yet, in these moronic modern times, doubt arises in my mind,
I look around by beach and mere, are those Eastern men still there?
Lifeboats embrace the wild, wild sea with volunteers so brave
I am reassured that our Eastern men
Still ride the Anglian wave!

G Hagan

The Quiet Life

When we moved to Lowestoft twenty years ago,
   We settled in from the town life we'd known.
My wife and I were ready for a slower pace of life,
   Free from all previous strife.
That's been replaced by three lovely children, I know,
   Even if we do nearly come to blows!
They're children of which we're justly proud,
   They've made their way amongst the crowd.

Lowestoft is indeed a lovely town,
   We can walk the streets without a frown,
The smell of a newly mown field,
   Gives such a high yield.
At times like this my heart is fit to burst,
   I know this isn't the first!

We have a beautiful beach,
   Bright as a peach.
This, we know many visitors come to see,
   If they didn't I'd say it was me!
The pavilion is a very imposing building, we know,
   It's not feelings we often show.
The amusements are as good as any seaside town,
   At least that's what my friends and I have found.

When visitors have gone and the nights draw in,
   I think of relatives and close kin.
I must pay them a visit, see how they are.
   Thank heavens we can rely on the car!
Christmas is the next family gathering,
   That should go with a fling!

J Amer

The River Nene

In Northamptonshire flows the river Nene
Years ago it ran clear and clean,
Many pronounced it Nene, others Nen
This river was special to us then.
At holiday times and most weekends
Young people gather at the river bend,
And on that wonderful river bank
We would offer up our thanks.
On that bank we'd eat our picnic
Pick lots of daisies and make chains,
Boys and girls altogether
Would take part in various games.
There in that lovely clean river
Some would paddle, others would swim,
All of us enjoyed ourselves
My memory has not grown dim.
These years are now in the past
Long before we heard about pollution,
Or may be we were very young
And not so easily disillusioned.
Lost in the memories of childhood
When everything seemed all right,
There in the middle of Northamptonshire
God's earth was always bright.

Dorothy Cornwell

Shake Up of Spring

Spring has surprised us, the winter has fled.
Crocus and daffodil are raising their head.
Meek little violets so gently emerging
Together with pansies on greensward converging.
Primrose a-peeping from under the hedge,
Plant pots appearing on each window ledge.
Even the birds are all celebrating,
Thrushes and blackbirds have started their *dating*
Soothingly swaying on bush, branch and stem,
Gladly greeting each other as Robin to Wren.
The famous dawn chorus is now in full swing,
Clear as a bell, their messages ring.
Take heed from the birds and the beautiful flowers,
Life still has its sunshine, in spite of its showers.
So dance to the melody, march with the band.
How lucky we are to live in this land.

Nancy Shanks

Suffolk Serenity

The peace of utter silence
Surrounds me as I gaze
Upon the Suffolk countryside,
Pulsating surrealism thro' the summer haze.

My vision absorbs such beauty
Almost incomprehensible to bear,
Unique virility of Nature,
Rural air so pure and clear.

I gaze upon the cornfields
Resplendent in golden hue,
Adorned with scarlet poppies
And cornfields of azure blue.

I seem to hang suspended
Between silent Earth and sky,
Envious of cotton wool clouds
Which beckon me, pensively I sigh.

The stillness is gently broken
As thrush and blackbird sing
And o'er the verdant meadows,
Concordant church bells ring.

The old church stands majestically
Guarding homestead, farm and inn,
Awaiting the harvest thanksgiving
In time-honoured Suffolk tradition.

Malcolm F Andrews

Grantham - My Kind of Town

Have you walked beside the Witham on a summer morn?
Watched the sun rise from the hills and hollows at dawn?
Swayed with St Wulfran's spire gazing at it from below?
Looked down on the town from Hall's Hill, rosy in the glow
Of an evening with the sunset setting western sky alight?
Heard the song of birds before they settled for the night?
Have you watched the busy bees outside the Beehive Inn?
Studied the architecture of The Angel, suffered the sin
Of massive destruction of the old historic George,
Waited to see from the ruins what modern man will forge?
Have you walked around the streets of this lovely ancient town?
Admired the old buildings which, so far, have not been taken down?
And more than this, in the dead of night
Have you gone outside in the bright starlight?
With the still, warm air sweet with scent of flowers
Breathed deeply ignoring the sleepless hours?
With no roar of traffic passing by
Have you then gazed up at the starlit sky
Seen stars so bright, so big, so near?
They could be plucked by hand it would appear.
Just a little part of the Grantham I know
I worry about the changes and so
I treasure the memories, special moments of awe
And pity the people who call Grantham a bore!

E A Collins

143

Waiting

It was partly autumn, the church
stood in the soft breeze.
I stood still, as I waited in the wind.

Tears dampened my face, as I
remembered you, as you once were.
The breeze lifted my frock, here
and there. Trees rustled
violently in the wind, sending
ruffled leaves here and there.

I wonder where you are now, for
soon I shall be with you, I shall
join you again wherever that may
be.

R J M Campion

Suffolk's Seasons

Snowfall, muffling the sounds of the life
That is unseen, but active. Small creatures
Hidden, waiting, hunger for the thawing.
Winter pale dawn sun breaks the dark. The wife
Peers through the pane, tries to see features
Of familiar things. For spring she's longing.

Trees, with their branches dressed in palest
Green chiffon, their roots warming the dark earth
To welcome the golden daffodil.
Spring sunlight sparkles, like a merry jest.
Yet May must come and go, ere our mirth
Is safe, from Jack Frosts bitter. swift, white kill.

Suffolk in summer, with drowsy bees
Dipping into perfumed cups of honey,
The golden pollen covers them all.
Men and girls in shorts, show winter white knees,
Today the world is theirs, no money
Is needed, to share this fizzy high-ball.

Fruit, ripe and sweet, now that winter's nigh,
Drops to the waiting hand. The days go fast,
And nights grow colder. Birds fly away,
Sewing black stitches across the blue sky.
Fires are lit and grey smoke plumes, drift past
The falling brown leaves, of autumn's last day.

Gwen Lewis

145

Evening Walk Near Oundle

We passed and stunted trees
In the dappled apple orchards
Fell about laughing,
Twisting and turning
In silent mirth.
Shaking pink confetti
From lovely heads
Dipping and swaying,
Playing pitch and toss
With the swirling breeze.

We heard wild birds chatter
Beside the dark lake
And a neurotic blackbird,
Clattered a warning.
Silver throated thrushes
Sang from silvered boughs,
And the gilded gander
Seeking fish for his young
Chased the black necked swan,
A grey squirrel
Cracked his last nut
And the trees fell about laughing.

Eunice Mary Carter

146

Essex Development Plan

Tentacles reach out,
The centre uncurls,
The dark stain of time
Sullies out.

Arms spreading northwards,
And eastwards and outwards,
She suckers inside
The sea's curves.

Seeking the wild lands,
The dark secret woodlands,
Nesting in hedgerows
Her young.

Her manicured starfish,
Straight-edged and sterile,
The poisoners' progress
Too fast.

Each tearing uncaring
Dust wearing is crushing -
Developed for whom
In the end.

Sara Bond

Ode to Norfolk

Froom Noorfook I do come
And royt proud'er that 'oy am,
There in't a better place than this
When all's sid'n done.

There in't no hills to break yer' back
Nor folk what put on graces,
An' I should know . . . born 'ere 'oy wus
And never left come 'ter that.

Fiona Thompson

The Sea

They ride like ribbons dancing through the air,
Each wave a different shape,
They ride up and down then peter out,
Waiting for another to take its place.

Every minute, every second a new wave runs along,
With only the fish to see them,
Such mystery we watched as we stood on the shore,
With all the sea before us.

Where do they go these ribbons so fine,
Where do they end there beautiful time,
Is there a grave yard for beauty such as thine,
Or is it something we will only see in time?

Christine Lawes

Abberton Reservoir

Like a sheet of glass the water lies
With ducks and coot, resplendent in feathers so smart,
A family of swans with their cygnets glide
And a heron stands poised, what a *work of art!*
Cormorants roost in a bare old tree
And stand there watching me, watching them, watching me,
Then with a quick movement away they fly -
Back at the shop with gifts to choose
What an array lies before my eye,
Just browsing around, I always loose
Myself, as books I spy nearby.
The hides are the secret place I go
To watch out for feathered visitors here,
The time slips by, the pace is slow
And cares fall away and disappear.
I can recommend a visit to this peaceful scene
To unwind and gently stroll along,
The wildlife carries on, regardless and serene
It will surely lift your heart to stir in song.

Rosina Rust

Life in our Village

Cottages of white are dotted here and there,
Sweet smells of the country as I breathe in the air,
Daffodils are dancing and swaying in the rain,
As I travel along and down the winding lane.

With fields for miles and dikes all round,
The trees so green and the twittering sounds,
In the distance I can see the church's weather vane,
To see such beauty is everyone's gain.

Smoke bellows out from the chimneys nearby,
Laughs and shouts from the women in the WI,
The clock on the church tower begins to chime,
Everything looks so quaint as the sun starts to shine.

As spring's in the air birds nesting in haste,
Flying back and forth leaving nothing to waste,
Sounds of the mowers being pushed to and fro,
People tending their gardens and using the hoe.

Summer's in full swing the fete's here once again,
With stalls and games we hope there's no rain,
So peaceful and quiet as we laze in the sun,
Just the lull of the tractors and kids having fun.

As the leaves fall in autumn and cover the ground,
People still chatter and gather around,
Meeting at the locals and the Post Office too,
Giving directions to those passing through.

Winter is upon us those dark freezing days,
As I look from my window through a dull misty haze,
Everything is so bare no people about,
Just wind, rain, sleet and snow not even a mouse.

Ethel McLean

Fenland Scenes

I see the fields across the fens,
alive with wavering golden corn.
There stands a crop of sugar beet,
where once had trod proud Roman feet.
A cobbled yard, with angry geese about to fly
at unwary strangers who may be passing by.

I see a grassy river bank,
where mallards bask in midday sun.
A watchful heron all alone,
so still, as though he's carved in stone.
A patient fisherman, pondering where to cast,
and reeds that gently sway as stately swans glide past.

I see sheep and cattle grazing,
and some old timber barns that lean,
Large stacks of see potato trays,
with implements from bygone days.
Rows of fragrant new mown hay, waiting to be spread,
and pens of hungry piglets squealing to be fed.

I see winding lanes and pathways,
and rooks in lofty elms above.
An ancient rustic wooden stile,
where weary travellers rest awhile.
Some far off brickyard chimneys, red and tall that seem
to rise and meet the clouds, then mingle in between.

I see white painted cottages,
with twisted shutters that creak.
The village school across the way,
and children laughing as they play.
A friendly old inn, which has *welcome* on the door.
And on the green a cross, for those who died in war.

David Wicking

Lincolnshire Lass

From the county of Lincs, I do be,
My family, mother, father, brother and me.
I'm proud to be a Lincolnshire Lass
Plain and ordinary, not rich.
I have no brass,
Country air, is fresh and clear,
Sights to see and behold.
Living in the country of Lincs
Is worth to me, any amount of gold.
The feeling of happy and contentment,
Is so precious and real.
I love living in the village of
Alvingham, Near Louth, Lincs,
It has real appeal.

Caroline Janney

Home

Lazy, hazy, sleepy Suffolk.
White puffy clouds, blue July sky.
Drifters leisurely take a stroll,
Cyclists and pony trekkers passing by.

Softly swaying cereals
Whisper to a gentle breeze,
Tickling, teasing eyes and noses,
Thus encourage that hayfever sneeze.

Orchestral insects buzz harmoniously,
Field mouse scurries, a bird swoops,
Another twitters, a hare races,
Darting fish glides, whips, turns in loops.

An artist captures the fresh green landscape.
Young busy stream matures into rippling pool.
Lovers picnic with Mother Nature
In shady woodland - dark, haunting, cool.

Industrious, dizzy, sporting county;
Economically growing year by year.
Arable farming, fishing and horseracing.
Pleased to boast such palatable beer.

Immaculate gardens, quaint old buildings;
Royal connections and home for the wealthy.
Place of great historic interest.
Good country air, clean and healthy.

Theatre, museums and sport for all,
Exquisite antiquities, markets and fairs,
Restaurants, cafes and traditional pubs.
Bustling locals buying and selling their wears.

Jacqui Fairley

Sea Mists

Sea mist writhes
Around Haven Corner tonight,
Filigree cobwebs
Hang from window ledges
As if to fasten me in the house.
An unearthly quiet can be heard!
It sparks a current in my imagination.

I see ghost ships
Sailing up the Haven,
I hear the tinkle of bells.
People say that years ago
A church sank into the sea.
Even the gulls are still,
The rat and the water-vole
Are safe in their own havens,
Not like me walking,
Shrouded in sea mist.

For a brief moment
The mist lifted,
The ghosts ships were yachts
Moored on the far mud bank,
The bells, the sound of rigging
Slapping against the masts.
My spark of imagination
Flickered and died
As I walked home
To my own safe haven
And was glad to be inside.

Pat Williams

In Essex

Weary windmills stand and dream
While waddling ducks abandon stream
And disregard the Highway Code;
To take the *kids* across the road;
Traffic queues a long way back,
Wonder what's upset the track:
Drivers bite their nails to bits:-
But no one minds because they're Brits.
Village greens with pubs attached;
Cosy cots, completely thatched,
Brilliant gardens neatly kept,
And streams, where by the willows wept.
In a place that's very near;
I've heard it said, 'Pooh bear lived here.'
His author's house, so small and round
In neighbouring village I have found.
Just along the lane from me;
A famous actress lived to be
A hundred years, when made a Dame,
And well deserved her claim to fame.
Yet further onward down the road
Stands a house, the past abode
Of Dodie Smith, whose inspirations
Wrote *The 101 Dalmatians.*
Ride South and East, you'll find a lot
Of sand and sea, when sun shines hot;
The *Golden Mile* and candy stick
And hats are pleading *Kiss me Quick.*
So in a nutshell, I'll just say,
'Give me Essex.' any day!

Patricia Woodley

Flat East

Flat
Flat with odd little lumps.
But still flat.

East Anglia
Flat.
East Anglia is flat.

Flat is not derogatory
It's not even an insult
Or a voice of contempt.
It's the truth;
East Anglia is flat
(and the Fens are the flattest of all).

But now honestly
Would you want it any other way?
Do you really want, mountains
And valleys,
Gorges and ridges
To disrupt those gentle, undulating slopes
(and those Fens, the flattest of all)?
Tell me, what is wrong
With a Flat East Anglia?

Tom Shepherd

Summertime

Summer breezes gently blowing
Stir the corn like waves on the sea,
In a meadow the cattle are lowing
While lazily drones the bumble bee.
Along the banks of a slow moving river,
Where graceful swans majestically glide,
In clumps of rushes thickly growing
Restless moorhens swiftly hide.
High in the trees that give them cover
A blackbird sings, a songthrush too,
And on the breeze wafted through the distance
The distinct call of the elusive cuckoo.
The scent of flowers floating on the breezes
No sweeter perfume will anyone find,
The sights and sounds of nature's graces
Tranquillise a restless mind.

Mavis Tofts

Ode to Our Church

Saint Mary's Church in Pinchbeck
Has stood proudly there for years.
It has seen a lot of happy times
But it's also seen the tears.
It's been a place for folks to go
And say a quiet prayer.
To take along their troubles
For it was always there.
The bells ring out to celebrate
The good news far and near
The people come to sing their hymns
It's really great to hear.
We marvel at the way our church
Was built so long ago
For everything's a work of art
The windows simply glow.
But now our dear Saint Mary's
Has troubles of its own.
It needs a major face lift,
Its body needs a tone.
So now it's up to all of us
To show what friends are for,
Lets dip into our pockets
And our loving church restore,
So please do make the effort.
Give all you can afford.
It will give you satisfaction
When you call to thank the Lord.

A Grunnell

Norfolk Natter

'The Fens are flat,
What do you make of that?'
Said Farmer William to Farmer Giles,
'They stretch so clear,
From far to near,
You can see for a hundred miles.'

'The Fens are flat,
It is true,' said Giles,
'No hills are to be seen,
And yet we pound,
Up and down,
In a tractor painted green.'

'The Fens are broad,
And oh my Lord,
They stretch from near to far,
And yet they seem to be agleam,
Do you really think they are?'

Farmer Bill replied,
'Yes the Fens are wide,
The horizon is quite hazy,
And the glow, you know,
Though it looks like snow,
Makes me feel quite lazy.'

'The Fens are still,'
Said Giles to Bill,
'Not a sound is to be heard,
And yet I hear,
Things crystal clear,
It really is absurb.'

Bill shook his head,
And softly said,
'Farmer Giles, you are quite wrong,
The birds have flown,
The wheat has grown,
Let's have another song.'

Jolyon Rose

Fenland Skies

What better to see than an evening sky
O'er fenland fields, whether wet or dry,
To stand out and watch the setting sun
In fiery splendour when day is done.

In winter the skies may be stormy at night
When myriads of stars are hidden from sight,
Distant horizons are outlined by dark clouds
A backcloth to buildings and bare outstretched boughs.

Calm days see the glowing sun sink to rest,
As a great ball of fire way out in the west;
The wonder of such a magnificent sky
Both gladdens the heart and pleases the eye.

When quiet calm follows the toil of the day
The barn owl ventures to seek his prey,
And swallows and swifts soar high and low
Enjoying the peace and the twilight glow.

The townsman may hanker for bright city lights
And pour scorn on others who savour such sights,
To the fenman tho' there is nowhere on earth
To compare with the fens, the land of his birth.

Lucie Gipson

Barrowby Stream

Soft rippling over sparkling pebbles,
Clear water reflecting changing clouds;
In a place of peace that nature sent,
Flows Barrowby Stream at the garden's end.

Gentle sounds of trickling water,
Chirruping birds and livening shadows;
The joy of a day that's newly born,
That's Barrowby Stream in the early morn.

Sycamore, Elder and Willows weeping,
Brushing the ground with branches sweeping;
Birds, fish, cool shade and butterflies
Flit happily here where nature thrives.

Low branches for horses, wellies for wading,
Small spades for digging and bushes to hide in;
A place of adventure for children at play,
That's Barrowby Stream in the brightness of day.

And as the sun sets and twilight arrives,
The first stars of night appear in the skies;
Birds quietly nesting, the butterflies 'way,
That's Barrowby Stream at the end of the day.

D M Fink